MY CURIOUS WORLD

First published in 2021 by Miles Kelly Publishing Ltd
Harding's Barn, Bardfield End Green, Thaxted, Essex, CM6 3PX, UK

2 4 6 8 10 9 7 5 3 1

Publishing Director Belinda Gallagher
Creative Director Jo Cowan
Editorial Director Rosie Neave
Senior Editors Fran Bromage, Sarah Carpenter,
Amy Johnson, Becky Miles, Claire Philip
Designers Craig Eaton, Rob Hale, Venita Kidwai, Joe Jones,
Simon Lee, Andrea Slane
Cover Designer Simon Lee
Image Manager Liberty Newton
Production Controller Jennifer Brunwin
Reprographics Stephan Davis
Assets Lorraine King
Indexer Michelle Baker (MHB Indexing Services)

ISBN 978-1-78989-119-5

Printed in China

British Library Cataloguing-in-Publication Data
A catalogue record for this book is available from the British Library

Made with paper from a sustainable forest

www.mileskelly.net

My CURIOUS WORLD

Words by Sue Becklake, Camilla de la Bédoyère,
Ian Graham, Anne Rooney and Philip Steele

Illustrations by Barbara Bakos, Tim Budgen, Ana Gomez, Leire Martín, Mike Moran,
Pauline Reeves, Daniel Rieley, Lucy Semple and Richard Watson

MILES KELLY

Contents

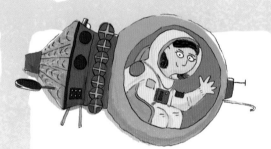

How many ASTRONAUTS
have walked on the Moon?

Answer on page 27

How **cold** is
NEPTUNE?

Answer on page 26

What is
THE SUN
made of?

Answer on page 12

Solar System

Words by Ian Graham

Illustrations by Barbara Bakos

Where is the Solar System?

It's all around you. The Solar System is the Sun, eight planets and everything else that moves through space with the Sun.

The planet we live on is called Earth. It's the third planet from the Sun.

Sun

In the middle of the Solar System is a star called the Sun.

Earth

Mercury

Venus

Planets

Planets are the giant things like the Earth that travel round the Sun. There are eight in our Solar System.

The four planets closest to the Sun are small worlds made mostly of rock.

Moons

A moon is a small world that circles a bigger object — usually a planet. Earth has one, and it is made of rock.

How do you make a solar system?

Our Solar System began as a huge cloud of gas and dust in space.

①

Dust and gas

How did the Solar System begin, and where did it come from?

First, an exploding star pushed against the cloud. The whole dusty cloud began to shrink.

③

So, there was a swirling disc of dust and gas – then what happened?

The dust and gas began to stick together, forming lumps that smashed into each other.

Lumps

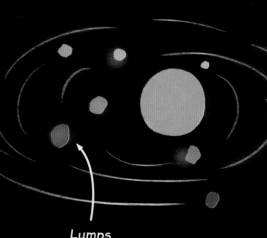

Is the Sun hotter than an oven?

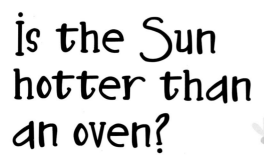

The Sun's surface is over 20 times hotter than a regular oven! The centre is even hotter — thousands of times hotter than an oven. It would melt the oven!

Surface

Core

NEVER NEVER look at the Sun. It's so bright and hot that it will hurt your eyes.

HYDROGEN

HELIUM

What is the Sun made of?

It's mostly made of stuff called hydrogen and helium. On Earth, hydrogen and helium are gases.

Why is the Sun bigger than other stars?

It isn't — the Sun is actually a small star. It looks much bigger than the other stars you see at night, because it is much closer to Earth than those other stars. They're all suns, but they are very far away.

Side-by-side with another star, I'm actually pretty tiny!

Scientists have found some suns that are 100 times bigger than the one in the Solar System!

Will the Sun be there forever?

No, but don't worry — it isn't going to disappear any time soon. The Sun should be there for another 5000 million years.

Where does the Sun go at night?

The Sun doesn't go anywhere – it's the Earth that is moving!

This spinning motion makes it look to us on Earth as if the Sun rises in the morning, crosses the sky, and then disappears at sunset.

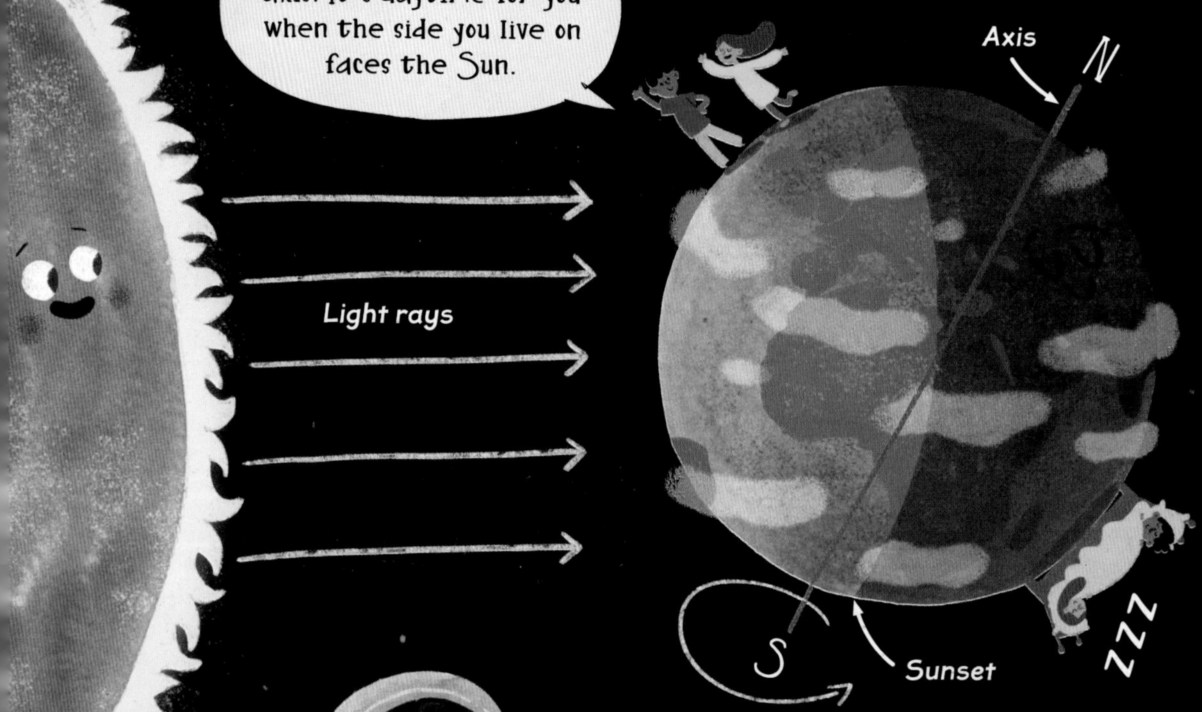

Our planet spins around an invisible line called the axis. It's daytime for you when the side you live on faces the Sun.

Axis

N

Light rays

S

Sunset

zzz

Why is a day 24 hours long?

It takes 24 hours for Earth to spin around once, and we call this a day.

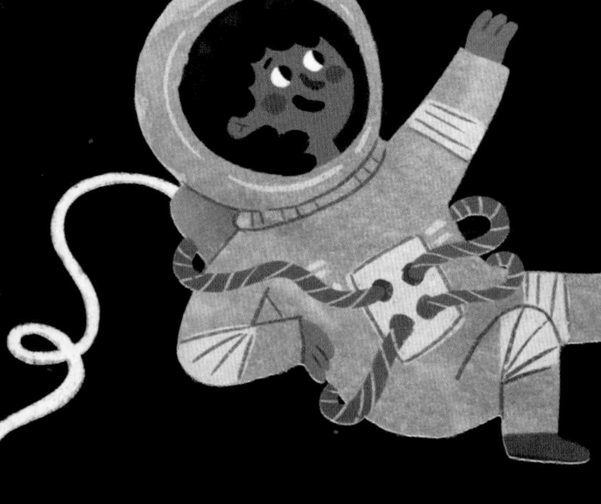

Why do we have seasons?

Because Earth's axis is tilted. This means different bits of Earth get the Sun's direct rays at different times during Earth's orbit (journey around the Sun).

What is the Equator?

It's an invisible line that circles Earth. It divides it into a northern (top) half and southern (bottom) half.

Equator

N

In June, it's summer in the north and winter in the south.

In March, it's spring in the north, and autumn in the south.

S

N

N

S

S

In December, it's winter in the north and summer in the south.

N

In September, it's autumn in the north and spring in the south.

S

What is a year?

A year is the time it takes for the Earth to complete one orbit of the Sun.

Did you know?

Jupiter has a huge storm called the Great Red Spot — it's about three times bigger than **Earth**.

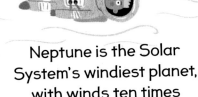

Neptune is the Solar System's windiest planet, with winds ten times faster than the worst hurricanes on **Earth**.

Saturn is famous for its rings, but **Jupiter**, **Uranus** and **Neptune** have them too.

My rings are easy to see, because they're made of pieces of ice. Sunlight bounces off the ice and lights them up.

The centre of the **Earth** is made of metal so hot that some of it has melted and turned to liquid.

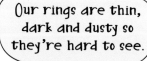

Our rings are thin, dark and dusty so they're hard to see.

You can jump six times higher on the **Moon** than you can on **Earth**.

Jupiter's moon **Ganymede** is the biggest moon in the Solar System — even bigger than the planet **Mercury**.

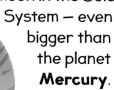

Dust storms are common on **Mars**. The sky there is pinky red, as so much red dust is blown about by the wind.

If you know where to look, you can see five planets without a telescope – **Mercury**, **Venus**, **Mars**, **Jupiter** and **Saturn**.

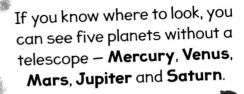

They are so far away they look like stars.

I'm only about half the width of the USA!

Astronauts who visited the **Moon** brought 382 kilograms of Moon rocks back with them.

Pluto was the Solar System's ninth planet – until 2006 when scientists decided to call it a dwarf planet instead.

There are between two and five solar eclipses every year.

Giant **Jupiter** spins so fast it has the shortest day of any planet – just 9 hours 55 minutes.

A solar eclipse happens when the **Moon** passes in front of the **Sun**. The Moon's shadow then moves across **Earth**, causing darkness to fall.

Are other planets like Earth?

Earth and the other three planets closest to the Sun are alike in some ways, but no other planet is exactly like Earth.

Why is it always so hot here?

Mercury is very hot because it's the closest planet to the Sun. It's smaller than Earth and it looks like the Moon.

Mercury

Why am I known as Earth's twin planet?

Venus

Venus and Earth are similar in size and structure — but the two planets look very different. Venus is wrapped in thick clouds of acid. They trap heat, so Venus is even hotter than Mercury.

Earth

Why am I blue?

Water covers 70 percent of Earth's surface. Sunlight contains all the colours of the rainbow. When sunlight shines on Earth, the water reflects the blue part of the light back into space.

Mars

Why am I called the Red Planet?

Mars is a small world about half the size of Earth. It looks red all over because its soil and rocks are full of rusty iron. Mars is a rusty planet.

What are the outer planets like?

The four planets farthest from the Sun — Jupiter, Saturn, Uranus and Neptune — couldn't be more different from Earth. They are giant worlds made of gas and liquid.

Jupiter

Saturn

Where did my rings come from?

How big am I?

Jupiter is the biggest planet in the Solar System. It's so big that more than a thousand Earths would fit inside it!

Uranus

No one knows.
They might
have come from
an icy moon that
broke up ...

... or they might be
ice left over from
making Saturn.

What's special about me?

This blue-green gassy world was the first planet ever to be found by someone looking through a telescope. It was discovered in 1781 by a man called William Herschel (1738–1822), who became famous overnight as a result.

What am I made of?

Neptune

Both Uranus and Neptune are made mostly of water, ammonia and methane, and it's the methane that gives them their blue colour. Jupiter and Saturn are made mostly of hydrogen and helium, like the Sun.

21

Would you rather?

Would you rather discover a new planet, like **William Herschel** did...

...or work out that all the planets in the Solar System orbit the Sun, like **Nicolaus Copernicus** did?

Would you rather live on **Earth** for your whole life, or spend your whole life in a **space station** where you could float about weightless?

If I lived on Mercury I'd be sixteen!

If I lived on Neptune I'd be younger than you!

Would you rather kick a ball really far on the **Moon** or make a red sandcastle on **Mars**?

Would you prefer to live on **Mercury**, where a year lasts just 88 Earth days, or on **Neptune**, where a year lasts 165 Earth years?

Which part of astronaut training would you rather do:

Work in a huge tank of water to practise **space walks**...

...or take a spin to get a feel for **extreme forces**?

If you had to name a new planet, would you rather call it **Aether**, after the Greek god of light, or **Erebus**, the god of darkness?

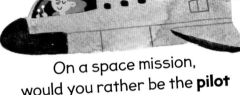

On a space mission, would you rather be the **pilot** flying the spacecraft, or a **specialist**, doing experiments and going on space walks?

Would you rather live on Uranus in **winter**, when the Sun doesn't rise for 20 years, or in **summer**, when it doesn't set for 20 years?

Would you rather slow down **Earth's** spin so days are longer, or move Earth closer to the **Sun** so that the weather is warmer?

What are shooting stars?

They're not stars! They're small pieces of rock that fly through space and into the air around Earth. Rubbing against the air heats them until they glow. They are also called meteors.

When lots of meteors appear in the sky, it's called a meteor shower.

Where do shooting stars go?

The smallest burn up and disappear. Others sometimes fall all the way down to the ground. If they land on Earth, they're called meteorites.

What happens when a big meteorite hits Earth?

It makes a hole in the ground called a crater. A famous crater in Arizona, USA, was made by a meteorite 50 metres across that hit the ground 50,000 years ago.

Why do comets have long, bright tails?

Comets are like giant dusty snowballs in space. If they fly near the Sun, some of the ice turns to gas and bursts out, carrying dust with it. The dust forms a tail that is lit up by sunlight.

How big are space rocks?

The biggest rocks in space are asteroids. Some can be up to 1000 kilometres across. Most asteroids are found in the Asteroid Belt between Mars and Jupiter.

How many?

-200° Celsius.

Brrrrrrrrrr!

The average temperature on the Solar System's coldest planet, Neptune.

178 moons have been found going around planets so far. More might be found in future.

Life appeared on Earth about **4,000,000,000** years ago.

7,500,000,000 The number of people living on Earth.

0 The number of moons that the planets Mercury and Venus have.

The Solar System is about **4,600,000,000** years old.

The Solar System's tallest mountain is Olympus Mons on Mars. It's nearly **3** times the height of the tallest mountain on Earth, Mount Everest.

How many astronauts have walked on the Moon?

12

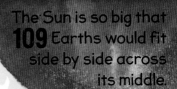

The Sun is so big that **109** Earths would fit side by side across its middle.

150 million kilometres: the distance from Earth to the Sun.

Halley's Comet appears in the sky every

76

years.

Just over **8** minutes: the amount of time it takes for sunlight to reach Earth.

165

The number of Earth years it takes the farthest planet, Neptune, to go once around the Sun.

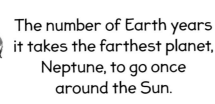

3

...the number of days it takes astronauts to fly to the Moon in a spacecraft.

There are **5** dwarf planets in the Solar System. They are called...

Eris   Pluto   Haumea   Makemake   Ceres

Is there life anywhere else?

Not that we know of — the search goes on. The spacecraft we have sent to other planets have been searching for signs of life there.

Erm... hello? Is anyone at home?

Why is there life on Earth?

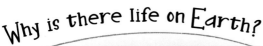

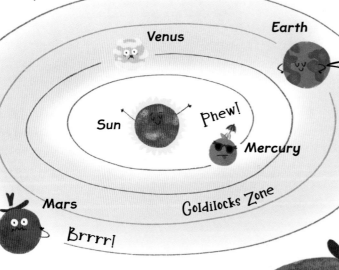

Venus

Earth

Sun

Phew!

Mercury

Mars

Brrrr!

Goldilocks Zone

My distance from the Sun means I have light, water and the correct temperature for life. I'm in what's called the 'Goldilocks Zone' — it's just right.

Why did people think aliens lived on Mars?

When people first used telescopes to study Mars they thought they saw lines on its surface. The idea spread that these were canals, made by aliens.

When spacecraft visited Mars, they found a dry, dusty planet with no canals — or aliens.

Is there water anywhere else in the Solar System?

Scientists think there may be oceans beneath the surfaces of some of Jupiter and Saturn's icy moons. Future missions will search for life there.

Europa

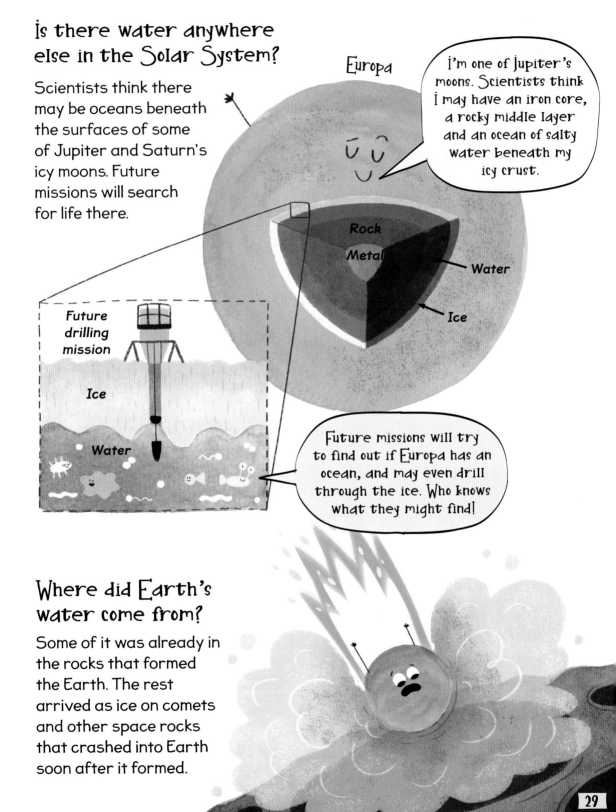

I'm one of Jupiter's moons. Scientists think I may have an iron core, a rocky middle layer and an ocean of salty water beneath my icy crust.

Rock

Metal

Water

Ice

Future drilling mission

Ice

Water

Future missions will try to find out if Europa has an ocean, and may even drill through the ice. Who knows what they might find!

Where did Earth's water come from?

Some of it was already in the rocks that formed the Earth. The rest arrived as ice on comets and other space rocks that crashed into Earth soon after it formed.

A compendium of questions

Why aren't planets square?

Planets are round because of gravity. This special force pulls everything inwards, forming a ball shape.

Why is Earth called Earth?

It comes from an ancient word meaning land. Earth is the only planet that wasn't named after an ancient Greek or Roman god.

Where is the best view of the Sun?

Standing on Mercury when it is at its closest to the Sun, the Sun would appear more than three times as large as it does from Earth.

Which moon is the weirdest?

Hmmm... maybe Saturn's moon Enceladus. It spews jets of gas and ice from its south pole!

Are there rainbows on the Moon?

Sunlight and rain are both needed for a rainbow. There is no rain on the Moon, so you will never see a rainbow there.

Why is the Earth's sky blue?

As sunlight travels through air, the blue part of the light is scattered in all directions, so the sky looks blue.

Can a spacecraft land on a gas planet?

No – and they can't fly through them either!
The extreme temperature and pressure
inside would crush a spacecraft.

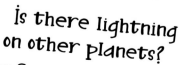

When did the first spacecraft go to the Moon?

In 1959, Luna 2 became the first
spacecraft to crash-land there
– no astronauts were
onboard.

Is there lightning on other planets?

Yes. Spacecraft have
seen lightning
storms on Venus,
Jupiter and Saturn.

Who is the Man in the Moon?

Some people think marks on the surface
look like a face. Others think they can
see the shape of a rabbit.

Are all the stars part of our Solar System?

No – the Sun is our only
star. All the others are
outside our Solar System.

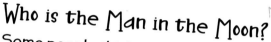

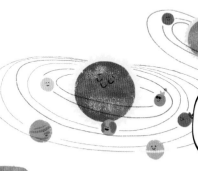

Many other
stars have their
own families
of planets.

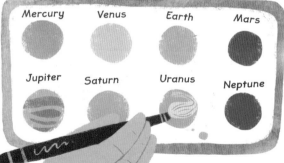

Mercury   Venus   Earth   Mars

Jupiter   Saturn   Uranus   Neptune

Why are the planets different colours?

Because planets are made of different
mixtures of rocks and gases that
reflect light in different ways.

Can CARS run on chocolate?

Answer on page 55

Why don't PENGUINS get frostbite?

Answer on page 47

Why do i need SUCH big ears?

Answer on page 46

Our Planet

Words by Camilla de la Bédoyère

Illustrations by Daniel Rieley

What is the Earth?

The Earth is a big, blue planet that travels through space. It is the planet we live on – in fact it is full of life!

> Animals and plants live on the land and in the oceans too!

Is there life on other planets?

Not that we know of. There are living things on Earth because there is air, water, warmth and light.

> It's night-time where the Earth faces away from the Sun.

Why is it dark at night?

As the Earth travels around the Sun it spins, too. This means sunlight can only shine on one part of the Earth at a time.

Polar bear

Penguin

South Pole

North Pole

Moon

People use telescopes and spacecraft to explore space. We've even landed on the Moon!

Reindeer

The Earth is facing the Sun so it's daytime here.

Lion

Why does the Earth need the Sun?

The Sun is a giant, hot star in space, and the Earth travels around it. The Sun gives us just the right amount of light and heat for plants to grow. Without the Sun, the Earth would be a dark and frozen planet, and nothing could live.

Is Earth like a jigsaw?

Yes, because it's made of pieces that fit together! The pieces are called plates and they are made of rock. The thickest parts of the plates poke up above the sea to form dry land, where we live.

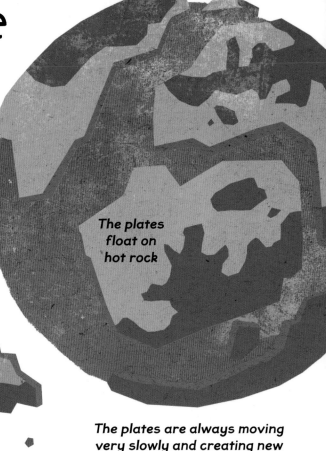

The plates float on hot rock

The plates are always moving very slowly and creating new land, seas and mountains

How do mountains grow?

Mountains are the tallest parts of the planet. Most of them grow when one plate moves and crashes into another plate. The rocks bend and fold, making mountains.

When plates move they can create earthquakes and volcanoes

How tall is the tallest mountain?

Mount Everest is the tallest mountain, and it is 8849 metres high. Everest is part of a group of mountains called the Himalayas.

Bar-headed geese are some of the highest-flying birds. We can soar over the Himalayas.

Mountain goat

Mountains are millions of years old, but some of the rocks deep inside the Rocky Mountains could have been made more than a billion years ago!

Snow leopard

What lives on a mountain?

Nimble-footed snow leopards chase mountain goats across slippery slopes. Life is hard on a cold mountain because there is often snow all year round.

CRASH!

Moving plates smash together

Hot rock

Did you know?

The loudest **thunderclaps** can shake houses and shatter glass windows.

If **Mount Everest** were at the bottom of the deepest ocean, its tip wouldn't appear above the water's surface!

More people have been to the **Moon** than have been to the deepest part of the **sea**.

The Earth's **plates** move very slowly — sometimes as little 2 centimetres in one year.

Bees can see colours in **sunlight** that are invisible to us, but they can't see red!

When **moonlight** is bright enough you might see a rainbow. It's called a **moonbow**.

Because of the way the world spins, you would weigh less if you were at the **North Pole** or **South Pole**!

If you took off in an **aeroplane** at breakfast time on Monday, and flew all around the world, you could be home for lunch on Wednesday!

We have just one **Sun**, but in outer space there are at least 200 billion more suns!

The centre of the **Earth** is hotter than the surface of the Sun.

Huge piles of bat **poo** can collect in caves where bats sleep. The poo is so smelly that the gas it gives off can kill animals that want to move in.

Big lumps of burning rock can explode out of a **volcano**, flattening anything they land on.

Planet Earth is a giant **magnet**. Animals such as bar-headed geese use the Earth's magnetism to find their way when they go on long journeys.

The mega-hot conditions deep inside a volcano make water boil so hard that layers of solid **gold** can form!

The Andes are the longest chain of **mountains** in the world. They pass through seven countries!

When the world's deepest lake **freezes** the ice can be more than one metre deep. Cars can drive on it!

What is the water cycle?

The way that water moves around our planet is called the water cycle. Most of the world's water is salty.

Sun

Clouds start to form

Water vapour rises

Water is all around us, even when we can't see it. It's not just in the sea and rivers. It's also in the air and in the ground.

Salty water in the ocean warms up and turns into water vapour, a type of gas. This is called evaporation. The salt stays in the ocean.

People use fresh water to drink, cook, wash, grow their crops and give to their animals.

Water vapour cools and turns to liquid water and falls as rain or snow. It is freshwater, which means we can drink it.

Some water flows through the ground

Water flows downhill, in rivers

Hydroelectric dam

River flows to the sea

How can a river power a town?

A river can power a town when it flows through a hydroelectric dam. The water passes through special machines that turn the river's energy into electricity.

What is the Equator?

The Equator is an imaginary line that cuts the Earth into two halves. Near the Equator, the weather is hot and sunny most of the time.

Arctic Circle

NORTH AMERICA

EUROPE

I am a jaguar, and I live in the tropical Amazon rainforest in South America.

The Sun shines strongly around the Equator, and there is daylight for 12 hours a day, every day.

Equator

SOUTH AMERICA

I am an emperor penguin and I live on frozen Antarctica with lots of other penguins, seals and birds. This is the coldest place on Earth!

Where does the Sun shine at midnight?

During the summer months in the far north of the world, the Sun doesn't set. In places such as Canada, Alaska, Russia, Greenland, Norway and Sweden the Sun can be seen in the sky at night. But in winter it is cold and dark all the time.

I'm a polar bear, and I live in the far north on the Arctic ice. I love eating seals!

I'm a tiger and I love the rain. I live in tropical forests of India, and I'm a very good swimmer.

ASIA

AFRICA

What is a rainy season?

Tropical places near the Equator are hot and humid. Strong winds called monsoons bring wet weather in summer. This is called the 'rainy season'.

OCEANIA

ANTARCTICA

How many?

1 The number of years it takes the Earth to travel once around the Sun.

24

The number of hours in a day... because it's the number of hours it takes for the Earth to spin once.

365

The number of days in a year.

About **50** volcanoes erupt every year on Earth.

One of the thickest blankets of snow ever measured was **9** metres deep. That's as tall as three elephants standing on top of each other!

The sea freezes over near the North Pole in winter. The ice can be more than **3** metres deep in some places.

The deepest part of the World Ocean is called the Mariana Trench. It's about **10** km deep!

2 The number of summers enjoyed by Arctic terns every year. These white birds fly all the way from the Arctic to the Antarctic to get the best weather!

It takes about **1000** years for a drop of water in the World Ocean to flow once around the Earth.

In one year, **10,000** millimetres of rain can fall in a tropical rainforest, while less than one millimetre falls in the driest deserts.

1.3 million Earths could fit inside the Sun.

Earth is about **4.5 billion** years old.

In the Antarctic, around the Earth's South Pole, temperatures can drop to **–50°** Celsius, or even lower.

In the last **50** years about one third of all Earth's rainforests have been cut down.

No one knows how many different types of animal there are on the planet, but it could be as many as **10 million**.

Are all deserts hot?

No, a desert can be hot or cold, but it's a dry place because it rarely rains. More rain falls in the hot and sandy Sahara Desert than in Antarctica, which is a frozen, windy desert that's covered in snow!

Hoodoos

Pillar

Arch

Why do desert rocks look so weird?

The wind picks up desert sand, and blasts it against the rock. Over time it carves out some amazing rock shapes such as hoodoos, pillars and arches.

Why do i need such big ears?

Those big ears help a fennec fox lose excess heat in the Sahara Desert. They're also good for listening out for burrowing bugs under the sand.

Why don't penguins get frostbite?

A penguin's body is suited to life at the Antarctic. Its thick feathers are like a waterproof blanket, and warm blood travels through the bird's feet so they don't freeze.

Penguins hold their eggs on their feet to keep them warm

Oasis

What's an oasis?

An oasis is a place where water can be found in a hot desert. It's one of the few places that plants can grow.

We're Bedouin people. We live in tents so we can take our homes with us when we travel to find an oasis, or food to eat.

Does it rain every day in a rainforest?

It can do! Rainforests are found in tropical areas around the Equator. The Amazon Rainforest is the largest rainforest in the world. It's in South America and is home to millions of animals and plants, from tiny ants to giant trees.

Monkeys and parrots feast on the tropical fruits

Why are plants important?

Animals need plants to survive because plants make oxygen. It's in the air, and we breathe it. Plants are also food for us and many other animals. When plants die they rot and turn into soil, which we use to grow more plants.

Rainforest plants have giant leaves and they grow flowers all year round.

The forest floor is home to fungi, frogs and billions of ants and other bugs

Trees grow tall and straight to reach the sunlight

It can be noisy in a rainforest. Birds sing, insects buzz, and howler monkeys like me call and whoop to each other!

Lizards and snakes hunt insects

Silent jaguars creep through the dark shadows or hide high up on branches

Morpho butterfly

Lianas are climbing plants that have long, bendy stems and dangling branches

Would you rather?

Would you rather search for aliens in **space**, or travel to the bottom of the **sea** and discover freaky fish?

If you were frozen water, would you prefer to be a **snowflake** or an **icicle**?

Would you prefer to be as tall as a **mountain**, or as colourful as a **rainbow**?

Would you rather swing like a **monkey** or swim like a **fish**?

What type of boat would you like to be in right now...

...a canoe on the **Amazon River** or a sailing boat on the **Atlantic Ocean**?

Would you prefer to dig for **diamonds**...

... or **dinosaur** bones?

If you lived somewhere else would you prefer to live in the desert like a **fennec fox**, or in the Arctic like a **polar bear**?

If you could be a plant would you choose to be a giant **rainforest tree** or a prickly **cactus**?

What do we get from the Earth?

We get lots of things from the Earth! They are called natural resources. Animals and plants are used for food and clothing. We use metals and other minerals to make things. We can even use wind and water to give us power.

Plastics are strong and waterproof. They are often made from oil, which comes from the remains of tiny animals that once lived in the sea.

Glass is made from sand

My bike is made of different materials that are found on Earth.

Rubber is a bendy, stretchy material that comes from rubber trees

Rocks are made of different materials called minerals. Metals such as gold and silver are minerals. Most sand is a mineral called quartz.

Metal

Fossil

Some fabrics are synthetic, which means they are made from oil or other chemicals

Metal is hard, shiny and strong. It doesn't bend easily. Metal comes from rocks that were made in the Earth's crust.

Rubber trees

Pencils and paper are made of wood, which comes from trees

Sheep fur is called wool and it is used to make fabric

Some fabrics are natural and they are made from plants or animal fur

Diamonds

Where do diamonds come from?

Diamonds are a type of mineral that forms deep below the Earth's crust. Diamond is the hardest natural material, but it can be cut to make sparkly precious crystals or 'stones'.

A compendium of questions

Will the Earth last forever?

Earth has been around for 4.5 billion years already but it's still very young for a planet, so there's no need to panic!

i'm still just a teenager planet!

Why don't we fall off the planet as it spins through space?

Thankfully, a special force called gravity keeps us on the Earth. It's a type of 'pull' force and the Earth, being heavier than us, pulls us towards its centre.

Can snakes live in the Antarctic?

There are no snakes in the Antarctic — snow and ice make it too cold. Snakes keep their bodies at the same temperature as the air around them, so they would freeze to death. They need warmth!

Why did my bike go rusty?

Bikes are made with a metal called iron. If iron gets wet (when it rains) the oxygen in the water joins with the iron to make a new material called iron oxide, or rust.

Why do planes fly above clouds, not below them?

When planes fly, air pushes against them as they move forward. This is air resistance. Air is thinner above the clouds, so there's less resistance, making it easier to fly, and so use less fuel.

What time is it at the North Pole?

It can be any time you like! During the deep winter there is no day, and in the middle of summer there is no night, so 'time' doesn't mean the same thing at the Poles!

NORTH POLE

Always time for ice cream though!

What is a tsunami?

It's a giant wave that hits land and destroys everything in its path. At sea, the tsunami isn't too high, but as it nears land, the wave may be 30 metres high. It's caused by an earthquake under the seabed.

Can cars run on chocolate instead of petrol?

Yes! Chocolate comes from cacao trees and it can be turned into a type of fuel called biofuel. Biofuels are cleaner than petrol, so that's good news (but a terrible waste of chocolate!).

Which other PLANETS have moons?

Answer on page 78

is it COLDER at the MOON'S poles?

Answer on page 80

Could the MOON crash into the Earth?

Answer on page 81

The Moon

Words by Anne Rooney

Illustrations by Ana Gomez

What is a moon?

A moon is a rocky body that orbits (moves around) a bigger object. Most planets in our Solar System have moons. Earth has one, which we simply call 'the Moon'.

I'm an artificial satellite, put into space by humans.

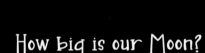

Moon's orbit

Anything that orbits a planet regularly is called a satellite. I'm a natural satellite.

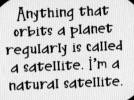

The Moon

Axis

Direction of the Moon's spin

How big is our Moon?

The Moon is small enough that it would fit inside Earth fifty times over. It's still the fifth biggest moon in the Solar System, though!

Does the Moon move?

It orbits Earth, and it moves with Earth around the Sun. The Moon also spins, turning on its axis (an imaginary line through the centre). It takes the same amount of time to turn once on its axis as to orbit Earth once (about 28 days).

The Moon   *Distance between Earth and the Moon, to scale*

The Moon is kept in orbit by gravity, a force that draws objects with mass towards each other. The pull of my gravity keeps the Moon from escaping into space.

Earth

Axis

Direction of Earth's spin

Is it far away?

Pretty far! The Moon is about 384,400 kilometres away from Earth. But it doesn't travel in a perfect circle, so sometimes it's a bit further away and sometimes a bit closer.

☐ = 10,000 kilometres

Earth

Where did the Moon come from?

It formed 4.5 billion years ago, when Earth was very new.

Early Earth

Theia

WHiZZ!

① A planet about the size of Mars, which has been named Theia, smashed into Earth.

② The energy of the crash melted a large amount of rocky Earth and Theia, and mixed them together.

CRASH!

3. Some of the molten (liquid) rock fell back to Earth and became part of our planet, but some was thrown out into space. It cooled, turning back into hard rock.

4. The bits of rock whizzed around Earth, bumping into each other. Eventually, all the lumps pulled together and fused...

...making me!

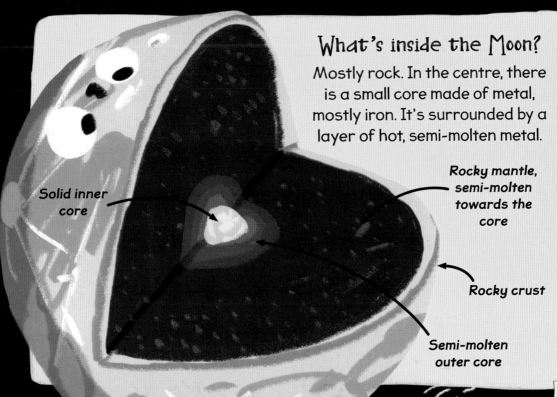

What's inside the Moon?

Mostly rock. In the centre, there is a small core made of metal, mostly iron. It's surrounded by a layer of hot, semi-molten metal.

Solid inner core

Rocky mantle, semi-molten towards the core

Rocky crust

Semi-molten outer core

Are there mountains on the Moon?

Yes! The Moon's landscape is made up of mountains, craters and flat plains. The surface is rocky, covered with a deep layer of dust called regolith.

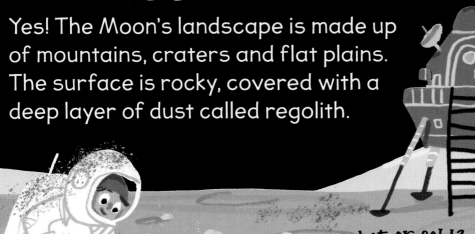

Is it hot or cold?

Both! It's scorching in the daytime when the Moon faces the Sun – it can be 127° Celsius. But it gets down to –173° Celsius at night. Daytime and night-time each last about two weeks, so any spot has lots of time to get hot or cold.

How can you jump so high?

Gravity is much weaker on the Moon, so people can jump easily and don't fall as quickly. A human can jump about 3 metres high and stay up for around 4 seconds.

Can you see the Sun and stars?

You can see the Sun in the daytime and the stars at night, just as you can on Earth. In daytime, the Sun is too bright for the stars to be visible. At night, the stars are dim as light reflected from Earth makes them hard to see.

You can also see Earth from the Moon, as long as you stand on the side facing Earth! It doesn't move across the Moon's sky, it hangs in one place all the time.

How many?

On the Moon, there are **500 million** craters that are more than 10 metres across.

Regolith on the Moon's surface is **2–8** metres deep.

It took Apollo 11 **51** hours **49** minutes to reach the Moon.

214
The number of known planetary moons in the Solar System.

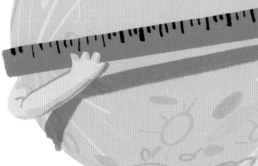
1737 The diameter (distance across) of the Moon in kilometres.

12
The number of astronauts who have stood on the Moon.

Neil Armstrong spent a total of **2** hours **12** minutes on the Moon's surface (outside the lander).

Eugene Cernan of Apollo 17 spent the longest time outside the lander, a total of **22** hours **5** minutes.

The Apollo 17 Moon buggy was driven the furthest, over **35** kilometres.

$25.8 billion The cost of the whole Apollo program ($194.3 billion at today's prices).

The Moon's gravity is **1/6** of Earth's gravity.

Ganymede

5268
The diameter in kilometres of the largest moon in the Solar System, Jupiter's moon Ganymede — it's bigger than the planet Mercury!

Mercury

The Apollo missions brought back **382** kilograms of Moon rock.

Why do we only see one side of the Moon?

The Moon takes as long to turn once on its axis as it takes to orbit Earth. This means the same side of the Moon is always facing us — this is called tidal locking.

Far side

Near side

North Pole

Near side

Sea of Showers

Copernicus Crater

Sea of Serenity

Ocean of Storms

Sea of Tranquility

Sea of Fertility

Tycho Crater

The dark patches are plains that were once covered by floods of molten rock. They're called seas, even though there's no water!

What is the far side like?

It's very different from the near side. The far side has many more small craters, and even craters within the craters. It has very few flat plains, and its colouring is more irregular.

Has anyone seen the far side?

It can only be seen in photos and from space. It was first seen by humans in 1968, when the Apollo 8 spacecraft went round the Moon. A Chinese spacecraft, Chang'e 4, landed on the far side in 2019 and took the first ground-based photos.

The huge South Pole–Aitken Basin stretches across almost a quarter of the Moon. Basins are massive impact craters.

Far side

Birkhoff Crater

Sea of Moscow

Hertzsprung Crater

Mendeleev Crater

Eastern Sea

Gagarin Crater

South Pole-Aitken Basin

Did you know?

The Chang'e 4 spacecraft grew the first plant on the Moon – a **cotton plant** – inside a special container. It survived for 14 Earth days.

An explosion during the flight of **Apollo 13** damaged the spacecraft, so the crew had to loop around the Moon and return without landing.

There are **moonquakes** (like earthquakes). Some are caused by Earth's gravity pulling at the Moon's insides.

Many spacecraft have orbited or landed on the Moon since I did!

The first spacecraft to land on the Moon was the Soviet craft **Luna 2** on 13 September, 1959. It crashed into the surface (on purpose!).

Footprints on the Moon will stay there unless disturbed. They are just slowly worn away by meteoric dust hitting the Moon.

As far as we can tell, **nothing** has ever lived on the Moon.

The Moon is slowly moving further from Earth, at a rate of about **4 centimetres** a year.

Bye!

Apollo 15 astronaut David Scott dropped a **hammer** and a **feather** on the Moon to show they both fall at the same speed when there is no air.

We were left behind to save weight for the return journey.

The 12 **full moons** of the year have names: wolf, snow, worm, pink, flower, strawberry, buck, sturgeon, harvest, hunter's, beaver and cold moons.

Astronauts left all their **personal waste** in bags on the Moon — and lots of other rubbish and bits of spacecraft.

Hoooooowl!

SERPENT SEA

The Moon's **plains** have names such as Sea of Cleverness, Serpent Sea and Sea of Waves.

Its **craters** include some named Billy, Carol, Mavis...

...and Bruce!

 This is how my phases look from Earth!

New Moon

Waxing Crescent

First Quarter

Waxing Gibbous

Does the Moon change shape?

It seems to change shape, but it doesn't really. As it moves around Earth, different parts are lit by the Sun. The changes are called phases.

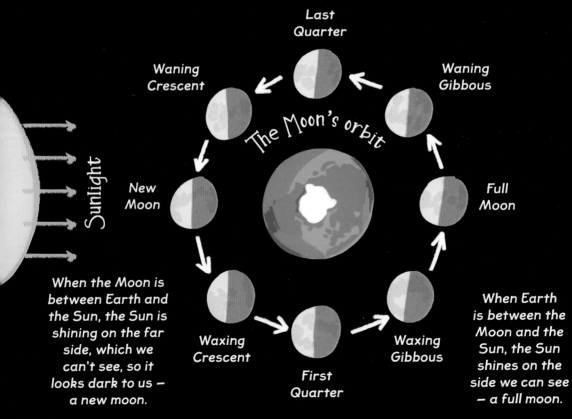

Last Quarter

Waning Crescent

Waning Gibbous

The Moon's orbit

Sunlight

New Moon

Full Moon

When the Moon is between Earth and the Sun, the Sun is shining on the far side, which we can't see, so it looks dark to us – a new moon.

Waxing Crescent

Waxing Gibbous

When Earth is between the Moon and the Sun, the Sun shines on the side we can see – a full moon.

First Quarter

Full Moon

Waning Gibbous

Last Quarter

Waning Crescent

I seem to shine because I reflect the sunlight that falls on me. I don't make my own light, like the Sun or other stars.

Why is the Moon sometimes red?

During a total lunar eclipse, the Sun is directly behind Earth and so the Moon is in Earth's shadow. Some of the sunlight passing through Earth's atmosphere is bent towards the Moon, turning it red.

Total solar eclipse

Can the Moon block out the Sun?

Yes — during a solar eclipse. When the Moon moves between Earth and the Sun and they line up exactly, the Moon's shadow moves over Earth. In some places, it blocks out the Sun completely for a few minutes — a total eclipse.

During a total solar eclipse, parts of Earth are plunged into darkness.

How does the Moon move the sea?

The Moon's gravity pulls at Earth's oceans. This makes the water pile up on the side nearest the Moon, creating a bulge. The water also piles up to make a bulge on the other side.

It's high tide here!

The bulge sweeps round Earth, pulled along by the Moon's gravity as it orbits, and also by Earth turning underneath. This creates the tides.

Low tide

Earth

Moon

High tide

Most coasts have two high tides a day, one when nearest the Moon and one when furthest from it.

What causes very high and low tides?

The Sun also helps make the tides. When the Sun and Moon are lined up (at full moon and new moon), they pull in the same direction. This creates extra-high and low tides, called spring tides.

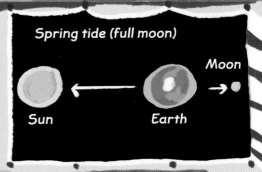

Spring tide (full moon)

Sun

Earth

Moon

Now it's low tide!

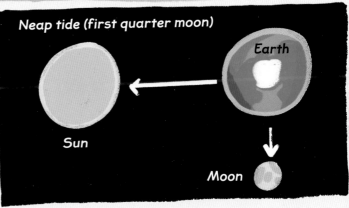

Neap tide (first quarter moon)

Earth

Sun

Moon

When the Sun and Moon are at right angles to each other, there are smaller tides than usual, called neap tides.

Would you rather?

Would you rather drive a **moon buggy** or be the **passenger**?

Would you rather visit the **far** side or the **near** side of the Moon?

To leave your mark on the Moon, would you rather write your **name** in the regolith or leave a **photo** of yourself?

Each Apollo mission landed in a different place on the near side.

Would you prefer to climb **mountains**...

Would you rather visit the **Apollo sites** or go somewhere **unexplored**?

Would you rather be the first person on **Mars**, or the first to go back to the **Moon**?

Which would you bring back from the Moon: a **rock** or an **Apollo souvenir**?

Did you enjoy your journey?

Would you rather find aliens on the **Moon** or be visited by aliens on **Earth**?

It's time for lunar sports! Would you rather see how far you can **throw** a ball or see how high you can **jump**?

Would you rather fly the **orbiter** round and round the Moon, or guide the **lander** down to the surface?

...or explore **craters?**

Could we live on the Moon?

We could build a Moon base that would provide us with air to breathe and a place to grow food, and protect us from the extreme temperatures.

Outside the base, we have to wear spacesuits at all times and breathe air from a tank.

Water could even be used to make rocket fuel!

Is there any water?

There is no flowing water, but there is ice, which could be melted. It is underground in rocks, and in craters near the poles. The craters are always in shadow, so the lunar water stays frozen.

The Moon doesn't have an atmosphere. It has a very thin layer of gases, called an exosphere. The mass of the exosphere is about 10 tonnes – the mass of two elephants. Earth's atmosphere has the mass of 10 quadrillion elephants!

Can I go to the Moon?

Not now – but if you become an astronaut when you grow up you might be able to. More Moon landings are planned, and we might build a lunar base to use as a stopping point on the way to Mars.

77

Which other planets have moons?

Mars has two but the other rocky planets, Mercury and Venus, don't have any. The gas giants, Jupiter and Saturn, and the ice giants, Uranus and Neptune, have lots — Saturn has at least 82!

Exoplanets — planets around other stars — probably have moons, too.

We're moonless!

Earth

Venus

Mercury

Mars

Jupiter

Are we all the same?

No, moons can be big or small. Some are icy and others are rocky. Some moons even have volcanoes that pour out ice or lava.

Why aren't all moons round?

Saturn

Moons come in many shapes — smaller moons are often not round. Gravity makes a moon round, but only if it's big enough.

Uranus

Some asteroids (rocks in space) have moons too!

Does anything live on other moons?

We don't know. Some moons have a sea of liquid water under the surface — they might be home to tiny, simple forms of life.

Neptune

A compendium of questions

How fast does the Moon travel?

It orbits Earth at 3683 kilometres an hour. It orbits the Sun at the same time, pulled along by Earth at 107,000 kilometres an hour.

How did astronauts go to the toilet on the Moon landings?

They had to use a special bag each time, as there were no toilets on the spacecraft.

Is it colder at the Moon's poles?

In places. The Sun is always on the horizon, and because of the Moon's uneven surface, some areas are always in sunlight and some are always cold.

How do we know what the Moon is made of?

Scientists have examined rock and dust samples brought back by the Apollo missions.

Was the Moon the same when dinosaurs saw it?

Can I see Moon rocks?

There are moon rocks in museums around the world, so there might be one near you. Museums also have meteorites from the Moon — lumps that have been knocked off and have fallen to Earth.

Could the Moon crash into Earth?

No. It would have to slow down enough to fall out of its orbit. Nothing could make it slow down that much.

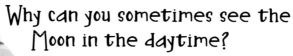

Why can you sometimes see the Moon in the daytime?

As Earth turns, every place faces the Moon for some part of the 24-hour day. You are more likely to see the Moon in daytime when it's close to a full moon.

The surface would have looked the same but it was closer, so looked bigger.

What colour is the Moon?

Grey. It looks white or yellow from Earth because it reflects a lot of light.

NO ZOOM!

What can you hear on the Moon?

Nothing — there is no air to carry sounds. A falling rock wouldn't make a noise, and a rocket wouldn't roar as it took off.

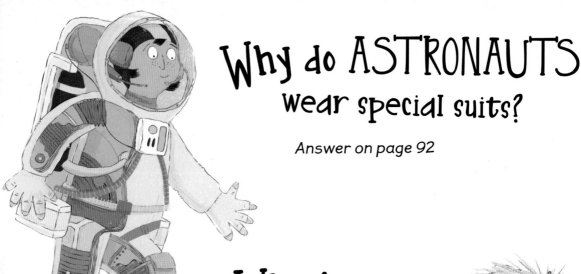

Why do ASTRONAUTS wear special suits?

Answer on page 92

What happens to astronaut POO?

Answer on page 107

How many ASTRONAUTS live on the INTERNATIONAL SPACE STATION?

Answer on page 110

Astronauts

Words by Sue Becklake

Illustrations by Pauline Reeves

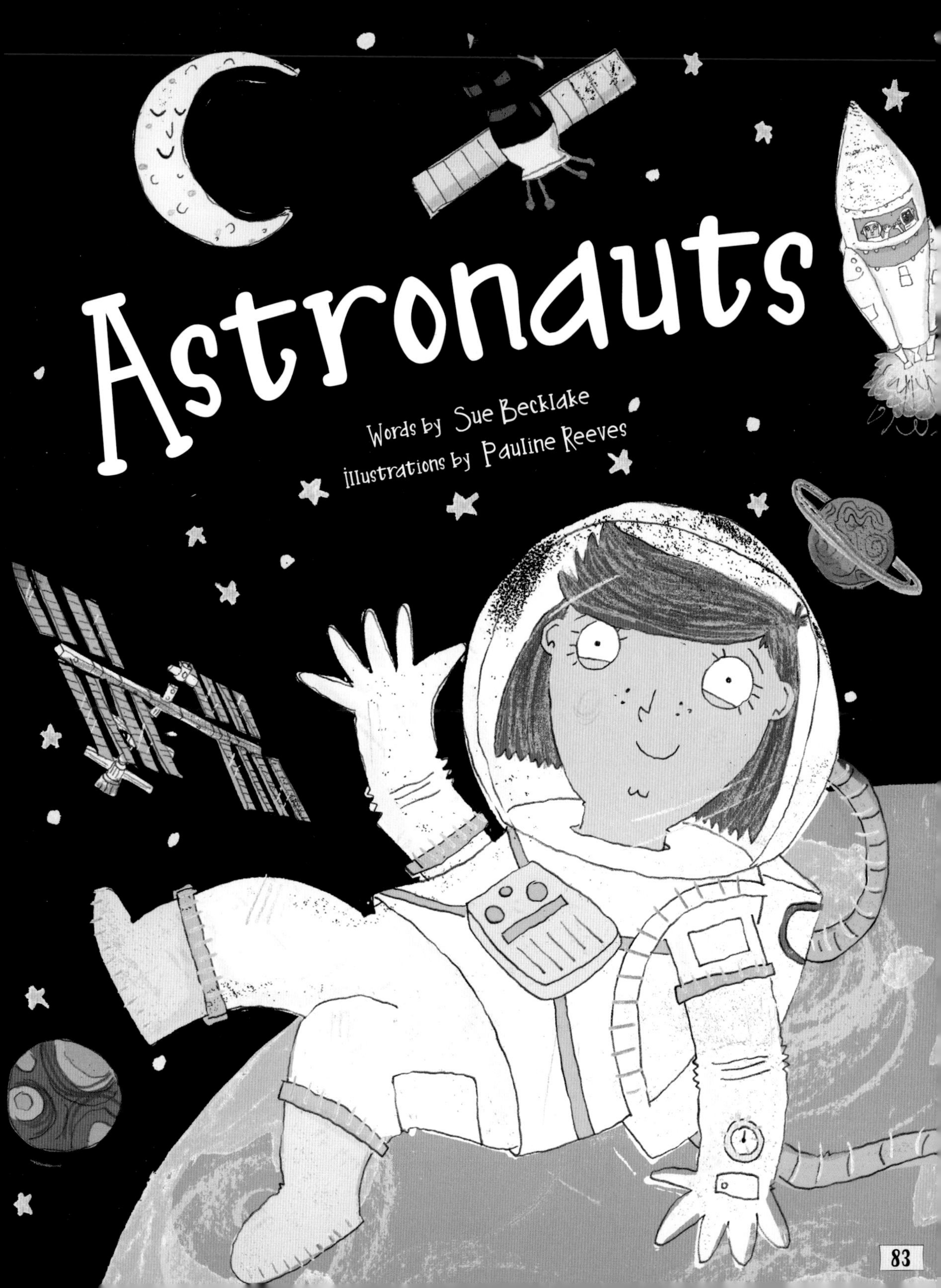

What is an astronaut?

An astronaut is a specially trained person who leaves Earth to travel into space. All around Earth, space stretches out between the distant planets and stars.

Astronauts are in here!

Moon

Rocket

Why do astronauts go into space?

To explore different places, such as the Moon, and to find out what it is like to live in space.

I am a cosmonaut, the Russian name for an astronaut.

How long do they spend in space?

Astronauts usually stay on the International Space Station (ISS) for six months, but four astronauts have spent over a year in space.

Most astronauts go to the ISS, which is 400 kilometres above Earth (less than the length of the UK). The furthest astronauts have been is to the Moon — 384,400 kilometres away.

Astronaut

International Space Station

Atmosphere

This is a layer of gases around Earth giving us air to breathe

Rocket launched from Earth

Earth

How do astronauts get into space?

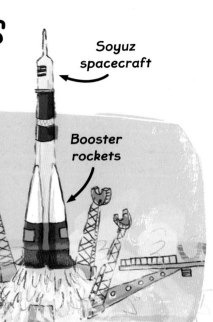

Soyuz spacecraft

① Launching into space

A huge, powerful rocket launches the Soyuz spacecraft, with three astronauts inside, into space.

Booster rockets

② Rocket separation

When the rocket is 50 kilometres up, its boosters separate. By the time it is 200 kilometres into space, the Soyuz spacecraft has separated from the rocket.

Boosters separate

③ Circling Earth

The astronauts sit snugly in seats inside the spacecraft as it orbits Earth.

Solar panels

④ Docking

The spacecraft catches up with the ISS and locks onto it. The astronauts can then climb on board to meet the ISS crew.

ISS docking port

⑤ Heading home

When the Soyuz spacecraft re-enters the air around Earth it is going extremely fast. The outside rubs against the air and gets incredibly hot, but the astronauts are safe inside. It's a bumpy ride though!

⑥ Safe landing

Astronauts feel nothing more than a bump when they land on the ground. They are helped onto recliners because their legs are weak after months of living in space.

Can anyone be an astronaut?

Any adult person who is fit and healthy can travel in space. Astronauts who go to the ISS have months of training, but in the future ordinary people will be able to go to space.

Now I know why they call this big plane the Vomit Comet — it makes me feel sick.

How do astronauts get used to floating in space?

In a big aeroplane flying in loops, trainee astronauts float for a short time as though they were weightless.

How do trainees practise spacewalks?

Wearing spacesuits underwater, they float in a huge tank. They can practise everything they will do when they go on spacewalks.

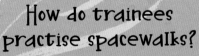

Vomit Comet

Aspiring astronauts need to be very healthy because there are no hospitals in space. They also need to know about science or engineering.

What special skills do they need?

Astronauts have to learn how everything on the space station works and how to fix it if it goes wrong. They also practise doing the experiments planned for their space trip.

Neutral Buoyancy Laboratory (underwater)

89

Did you know?

Astronauts built the **ISS**, joining the parts together in space.

Russian cosmonaut, Yuri Gagarin, was the **first person** to fly into space on 10 April 1961.

Between 1981 and 2011, American **space shuttles** carried astronauts into space. The shuttles flew many times, taking off like a rocket and landing back on a runway like a plane.

Spacewalking astronauts use a **tether** to fix themselves to the ISS so they can't float off.

You can sometimes see the ISS moving slowly across the sky like a **bright star** just after sunset.

Astronauts add **liquid** salt and pepper to their food. Grains or powder would float around and get into vital equipment.

The first person to walk on the **Moon** in July 1969 was Neil Armstrong.

Many astronauts get **space sick**, like travel sickness, but it soon wears off.

The first female astronaut, and the only **woman** to fly solo in space, was Valentina Tereshkova in 1963.

Peggy Whitson was the first **female commander** of the ISS in 2007 and 2016.

There have been **seven** astronaut tourists who have paid millions of dollars to fly to the ISS.

What do astronauts wear?

Inside a space station they wear ordinary clothes, but outside astronauts need a spacesuit to keep them alive. Spacesuits are very expensive – each costs about $12 million.

A backpack, called a Life Support System, carries oxygen to breathe and water for cooling

The helmet's gold visor protects the astronaut's eyes from the strong sunlight

I can talk to the rest of the crew using the microphone and earphones in my cap.

Astronauts sip drinking water through a tube near their mouth

92

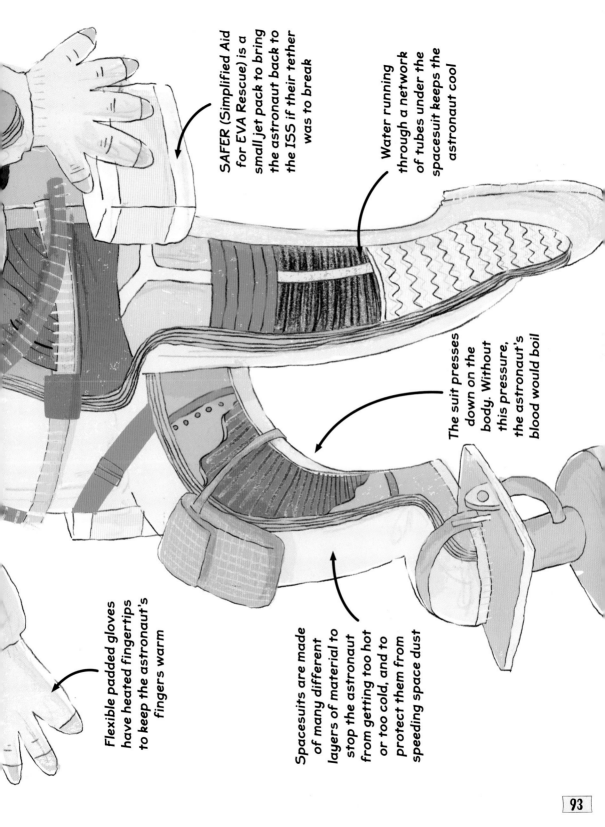

SAFER (Simplified Aid for EVA Rescue) is a small jet pack to bring the astronaut back to the ISS if their tether was to break

Water running through a network of tubes under the spacesuit keeps the astronaut cool

The suit presses down on the body. Without this pressure, the astronaut's blood would boil

Spacesuits are made of many different layers of material to stop the astronaut from getting too hot or too cold, and to protect them from speeding space dust

Flexible padded gloves have heated fingertips to keep the astronaut's fingers warm

Where do astronauts live?

The International Space Station, which is circling the Earth, is home to astronauts exploring space. It is made of sections called modules where astronauts can eat, sleep and work.

Does everything float in a space station?

Yes! On Earth, gravity pulls everything down to the ground, but in a space station, the astronauts and everything else like food, water and tools float around if they are not fixed down. We say they are weightless.

Docking area

International Space Station

How do astronauts get food and water?

Everything they need is delivered from Earth in a Soyuz spacecraft or a robot ferry.

Is it easy to sleep in space?

Not really! Astronauts fix their sleeping bag to the wall so they don't float around and bump into things while they are asleep.

Sleeping area

I wear earplugs and an eye mask to keep out the noise and light so I can sleep.

Living and sleeping area

Solar panels

Laboratory area

Where does the electricity come from?

Huge solar panels on the space station turn sunlight into electricity to run all the equipment.

Solar panels

95

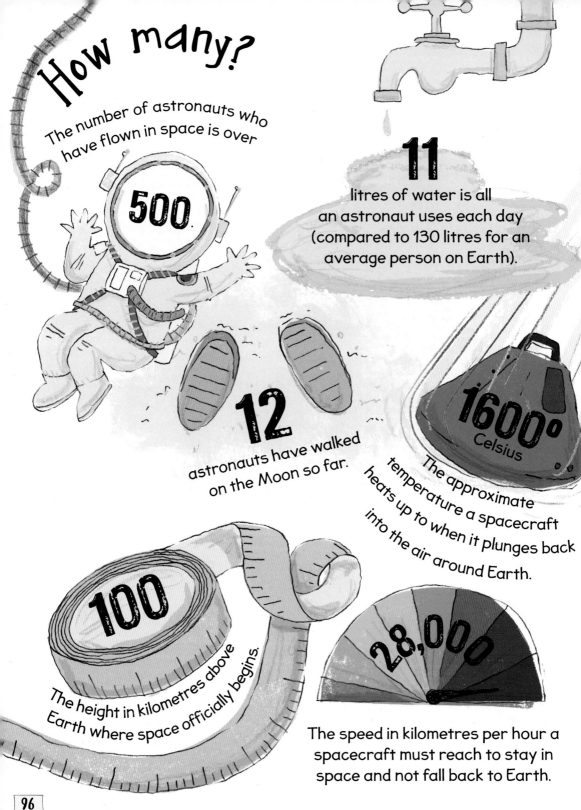

How many?

The number of astronauts who have flown in space is over **500**.

11 litres of water is all an astronaut uses each day (compared to 130 litres for an average person on Earth).

12 astronauts have walked on the Moon so far.

1600° Celsius The approximate temperature a spacecraft heats up to when it plunges back into the air around Earth.

100 The height in kilometres above Earth where space officially begins.

28,000 The speed in kilometres per hour a spacecraft must reach to stay in space and not fall back to Earth.

The ISS has a supply of about **2400** litres of water but over 90 percent of it, including toilet water and sweat, is recycled!

Astronauts from **18** different countries have lived on the ISS.

The oldest astronaut so far is John Glenn. He went into space at the age of **77**.

The number of days it took the Apollo astronauts to get to the Moon. **3**

A spacesuit backpack provides an astronaut with about **8.5** hours of oxygen and water, and enough nitrogen gas for the SAFER jet thrusters to power back to the ISS.

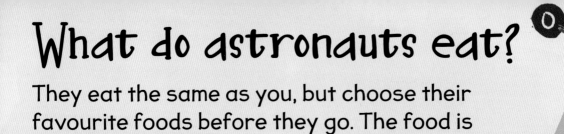

What do astronauts eat?

They eat the same as you, but choose their favourite foods before they go. The food is cooked on Earth and then sent to the space station in ready-to-eat portions.

Food is dried so it lasts longer and is lighter for the journey.

Adding hot water to this packet of dried food makes it into a tasty meal. The packet is fixed to my tray to stop it floating away.

Spaghetti

Cups are no good to us, because drinks float out of them. We add water to a packet of dried powder then suck the drink through a straw.

99

Why do astronauts exercise in space?

Exercise helps to keep the astronauts strong and healthy. Their bodies change in space without gravity to pull them down to the ground. They get taller, and their bones and muscles get weaker.

My space exercise bike doesn't have a saddle. A harness keeps me in place and my feet clip onto the pedals.

How much exercise do they do?

Two hours of exercise every day is enough to keep an astronaut's heart and muscles strong.

What jobs are done in space?

Astronauts are very busy. They look after the ISS, keep it clean and tidy, and repair anything that goes wrong. They also do lots of experiments.

> We monitor our bodies to see how we cope with weightlessness.

Who cleans the ISS?

Everyone helps to clean once a week. Astronauts use a vacuum cleaner to remove dust. They also check everything is working well and fix it if not.

> I'm using wipes and a cloth sprayed with detergent to remove any dirt.

> One day we may be able to grow most of our own food in space.

What experiments do astronauts do?

They try to find out how things, such as crystals and plants, grow differently in space.

What is an EVA?

Extravehicular Activity (EVA) is the name for a spacewalk. This is when astronauts put on spacesuits to work outside the space station, installing new equipment or doing repairs.

Do astronauts have robot helpers?

Yes! Canadarm2 is a robot arm on the outside of the ISS. Astronauts operate it from inside, and it can help to move or install bulky parts.

Why do astronauts take living things into space?

They study how things behave differently in space. They grow seeds, as well as watch insects and small animals to study how quickly they get used to weightlessness.

Would you rather?

Eeuww, stinky smells! Would you rather live in the **sealed** ISS or on Earth where you can just **open** a window?

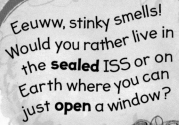

Would you rather **live** in a space station circling Earth or **travel** for six months to visit Mars?

Time for pooping practice! Would you prefer a **comfy toilet** at home or aiming at a teeny hole on a **space toilet**?

If you were working in space, would you prefer to **suit up** for a space walk outside or stay inside in **pyjamas** to operate a robot arm?

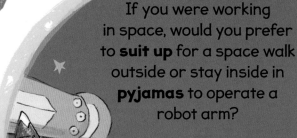

Would you rather watch spiders **spin webs** or ants **build tunnels** in weightlessness?

Would you prefer to float inside a **space station** or float around a **swimming pool** on Earth?

Would you rather play **golf** on the Moon (like astronaut Alan Shephard in 1971) or **table tennis** on the ISS?

Would you prefer to look down at **Earth** from the ISS or stare at the **Moon** from Earth through a telescope?

Can astronauts take a bath?

Astronauts don't bath in space, because water would not run out of a tap or stay in a bath. Water turns into balls of liquid that float around.

To wash my hair I rub shampoo and a little water into it, then use a comb and towel to remove the dirt.

Instead of taking a shower, I have washed myself with a soapy cloth and am now towelling dry.

How about having a shower instead?

The US Skylab space station in 1973 did have a shower. It was sealed shut to keep all the water inside and the astronauts had to vacuum up the water before they could get out.

How do they brush their teeth?

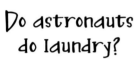

> I clean my teeth with an ordinary toothbrush, but use special toothpaste that I can swallow. There's no need to rinse with water.

Do astronauts do laundry?

Astronauts save water by not washing their clothes. They throw away their underwear and socks, but keep wearing the same outer clothes for about six weeks!

Space toilet

Where does their poo go?

Space toilets do not use water for flushing. Flowing air sucks the waste away into bags to be recycled or taken back to Earth. Astronauts have to fix themselves down so they stay on the toilet.

Will people ever visit Mars?

Yes, there are plans to send people to Mars. The journey will take six months each way. They will have to take everything they need to stay alive — food, water and air to breathe.

Command centre

Possible Mars colony

What would people wear on Mars?

Laboratory

I'd need a spacesuit to provide air to breathe, and to keep warm and safe from radiation and blowing dust.

Is there any water to drink?

There is no running water on Mars, but there is frozen ice that could be used near its north and south poles.

Could people sunbathe on Mars?

It would be far too cold! Mars is further from the Sun than Earth. It's also dry and windy, and there are often huge dust storms.

Dust storm

Wind energy generators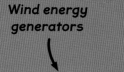

Radio communication building

Is the air on Mars breathable?

No. Humans need oxygen gas to breathe and the air on Mars is mostly carbon dioxide gas.

Living pod

Where could they live?

If astronauts built homes on Mars, they would need thick walls to protect against dangerous radiation. They might even build homes underground.

Living pod

A compendium of questions

How often do astronauts see a sunrise?

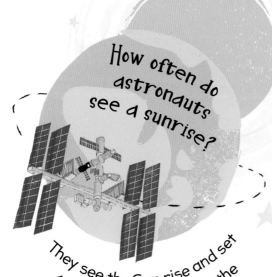

They see the Sun rise and set 16 times every day from the ISS as it circles Earth.

How big is the ISS?

The living space inside is bigger than a six-bedroom house. The whole station stretches out to about the size of a sports field.

How many astronauts live on the ISS?

Usually six, but there are nine when a new crew arrives.

How fast does the ISS travel?

27,600 kilometres an hour, about 30 times faster than a Boeing 747 jet.

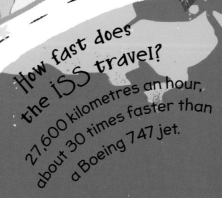

What happens to waste and rubbish?

They seal it in bags and put it in a cargo spacecraft, which either lands on Earth or burns up in the air.

Which countries have launched astronauts with their own rockets?

China, Russia and USA. Astronauts from other countries travel on US or Russian rockets.

Why do astronauts like spicy food?

Weightlessness can give astronauts stuffy noses, so stronger flavours taste better.

Who was Laika?

A dog — and the first living creature to orbit Earth in 1957.

When did the first astronauts go to the ISS?

In 2000 and there have been astronauts on board ever since.

How long will footprints stay on the Moon?

Millions of years because there is no air on the Moon to blow them away.

OPENING SOON!

What can ORBITERS do?

Answer on page 131

How do LANDERS land?

Answer on page 130

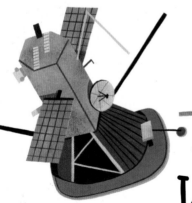

What is the fastest SPACECRAFT?

Answer on page 139

Space
Machines

Words by Anne Rooney

Illustrations by Lucy Semple

What are space machines?

Any machines that are sent into space! They include rockets, shuttles, satellites and probes.

i travel around (orbit) Earth and keep track of the weather.

Meteosat weather satellite

Hubble Space Telescope

Falcon 9 rocket

i look far into space and take photos.

Space starts 80–100 kilometres above Earth's sea level

I blast spacecraft from Earth into space.

Lunar Reconnaissance Orbiter

Do space machines come back to Earth?

A few come back to Earth after their missions, while others carry on working in space. Some are deliberately crashed into a moon or planet, or left behind there. The rest end up as 'space junk'.

I'm in orbit around the Moon right now!

International Space Station

I'm a large base in space where astronauts live and work.

Which was the first space machine?

The Russian satellite Sputnik was launched in 1957 and was the first satellite to orbit Earth. Sputnik started a 'space race' between Soviet Russia and the USA. The two countries competed to see who could achieve the most in space.

I was the size of a beach ball!

Which was the biggest rocket?

The Saturn V rockets used to carry the Apollo spacecraft to the Moon were the largest rockets that have ever launched.

How do rockets take off?

At launch, rockets stand upright. They burn huge amounts of liquid or solid fuel, which makes a lot of exhaust. This blasts out of the back of the rocket, pushing it upwards.

Crew inside Apollo spacecraft

Saturn V

Stage 4

Stage 3

Stage 2

Stage 3 falls away

Stage 4 goes off on its own!

Stage 2 falls away

Stage 3 fires twice – once to place the craft in orbit and again to send it towards its destination.

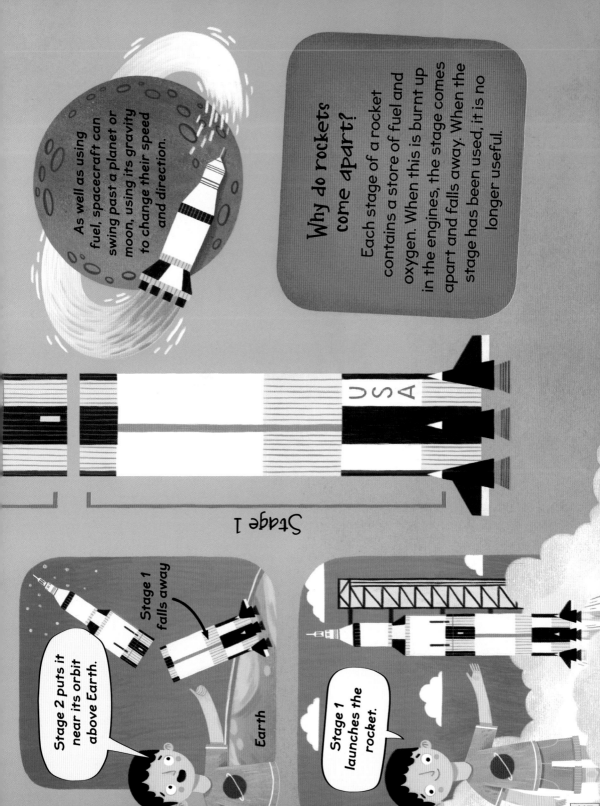

As well as using fuel, spacecraft can swing past a planet or moon, using its gravity to change their speed and direction.

Why do rockets come apart?

Each stage of a rocket contains a store of fuel and oxygen. When this is burnt up in the engines, the stage comes apart and falls away. When the stage has been used, it is no longer useful.

U S A

Stage 1

Stage 2 puts it near its orbit above Earth.

Stage 1 falls away

Earth

Stage 1 launches the rocket.

Who was the first person in space?

In **1961**, Russian Yuri Gagarin travelled into space in Vostok 1 – a tiny capsule launched by a rocket. It circled Earth once, taking 89 minutes, then came back down. Gagarin left the craft with a parachute.

Cosmonaut Yuri Gagarin.

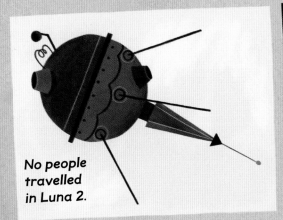
No people travelled in Luna 2.

How did Apollo land on the Moon?

After being launched by a Saturn V rocket, the Apollo spacecraft was pulled into orbit by the Moon's gravity. A lander then separated and went down to the Moon's surface.

Which spacecraft landed on the Moon first?

The Russian Luna 2 in 1959. Lots of spacecraft have been to the Moon since then, including six American Apollo craft carrying astronauts.

The service and command module stayed in space.

Who was first to walk on the Moon?

Me! I'm an American astronaut called Neil Armstrong.

And I was next. I'm Buzz Aldrin. We went together on Apollo 11 in 1969.

I'm Michael Collins. I stayed in the command module.

When the astronauts were ready to leave the Moon, thrusters blasted part of the lander back up into space to rejoin the service and command module.

This is much easier than walking!

The Moon buggy could drive over objects up to 30 centimetres high.

Did the astronauts have a car on the Moon?

Kind of! The last three Apollo missions in 1971 and 1972 took a Moon buggy to drive on the surface.

How many?

2.5 million
The number of parts in a space shuttle.

40,300
The speed in kilometres per hour a rocket needs to reach to leave Earth's atmosphere.

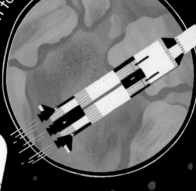

5
space shuttles were built and flew into space many times. There were **135** flights.

There are 8 layers in the Extravehicular Mobility Unit worn for spacewalks.

1 million
The number of people the technology company SpaceX hope to have living on Mars in 100 years.

1323
The total number of flight-days of the five NASA space shuttles over 30 years.

924,675
The number of litres of fuel used by the first stage of a Saturn V rocket.

10
space stations have successfully launched and been occupied.

0.14 The top speed in kilometres per hour of the Curiosity Mars rover.

18
The top speed in kilometres per hour of the Moon buggy.

There are **128 million** pieces of space junk one millimetre to one centimetre wide orbiting Earth right now.

Only **1** space station is still operational.

How are satellites placed in space?

Rockets and space shuttles have carried satellites into space. A rocket carries the satellite to the right height, then fires smaller rockets to adjust its position and release the satellite.

The Moon

I'm Earth's only natural satellite!

Why don't they float off into space?

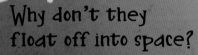

Satellites are held in place by Earth's gravity. They use thrusters to stay up as they start to slip towards Earth over time.

What are they used for?

Lots of things! Some satellites track the weather or your location, while others bounce radio waves around Earth to provide TV, radio and internet signals.

Weather satellite

Communications satellite

How big are they?

The smallest are CubeSats, which are just a few centimetres across and weigh less than an apple! The largest satellite is as big as a football field.

Would you rather?

Be the **first** human on **Mars**...

...or **first** to find a desert **island**?

Would you rather **discover** a new **planet** with a telescope...

...or **visit** the **Moon**?

What's better? A **holiday** on the International Space Station or **climbing** Mount Everest?

Would you prefer to invent a **spaceship** that could travel to Jupiter in one day...

...or a **flying car?**

Would you rather have a **rocket** or a **satellite** named after you?

...or your favourite **movie star?**

Who would you like to **meet** more, an **alien**...

Would you prefer to spend a day in **zero gravity**...

...or seeing **great white sharks** in the wild?

What's better? Going on a **spacewalk** or controlling the **space station?**

What is the International Space Station?

It's a research base in space. Built from modules arranged along a solid metal backbone, it is powered by solar panels. Astronauts live there for six months at a time.

Robotic arm

Solar panels

How was it built?

The ISS was built in space, from modules carried up separately by rockets and in the space shuttle. A robotic arm and astronauts bolted all the parts together.

How do astronauts get to the ISS?

At first they were carried by a space shuttle, which went to the ISS and came back to Earth. Now they go in a Russian Soyuz craft and return in its descent module.

International Space Station (ISS)

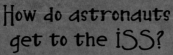

Space shuttle

Is the ISS speedy?

Yes! The ISS travels at 8 kilometres per second at a height of 360 kilometres. It covers a distance equivalent to the Moon and back every day!

What's life like on board?

It's not easy! There is zero gravity, so the crew float about. This makes eating, drinking, washing and going to the toilet more difficult!

Every day is a bad hair day in space!

Saturn

What are space probes?

Probes are unmanned robotic spacecraft. They go on long journeys to explore objects in space, including planets, moons, asteroids and comets. Some probes carry landers, which they release onto the surface of a planet or other object.

How are probes controlled?

By computer. Some of a probe's activities are programmed in advance while others are controlled from Earth. When a probe is far away it can take hours for radio signals to reach it, so it needs to make some 'decisions' itself.

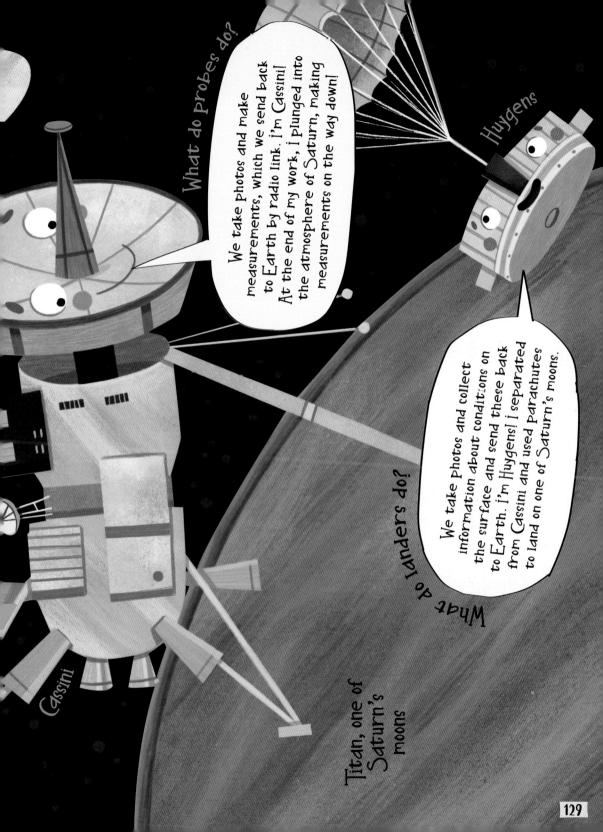

We take photos and make measurements, which we send back to Earth by radio link. I'm Cassini! At the end of my work, I plunged into the atmosphere of Saturn, making measurements on the way down!

Huygens

We take photos and collect information about conditions on the surface and send these back to Earth. I'm Huygens! I separated from Cassini and used parachutes to land on one of Saturn's moons.

What do landers do?

Cassini

Titan, one of Saturn's moons

129

Have spacecraft been to Mars?

By 2019, 56 spacecraft had set off for Mars and 26 had been successful. Some are still in orbit around Mars, while some landers are still on the surface.

Sky crane lowering Curiosity

I use thrusters to slow me down, and lower the lander on a strong cable.

How do spacecraft get to Mars?

A rocket launches the craft into space, points it in the right direction and lets go! It takes about 7—8 months to get to Mars and the trip needs careful planning, as both Earth and Mars are moving.

How do landers land?

They use thrusters pointing downwards to slow their fall to the surface. Thrusters push them upwards while gravity pulls them down. The Curiosity rover was lowered by a sky crane!

What can orbiters do?

Orbiters look down on the whole planet as they travel around it. They measure gases, temperature and the height of the land, and take photos.

Mars Reconnaissance Orbiter

My top speed is just 140 metres an hour!

Curiosity

Can rovers look for life on Mars?

Yes! Rovers are landers that can move around, gathering information from different places. They look in close detail at the soil and rock, and can look for chemical signs of life.

Have any spacecraft left the Solar System?

Yes! Two Voyager spacecraft have left our Solar System and are journeying into interstellar space (the space between stars). Voyager 1 has travelled the furthest.

Golden record

Will the Voyagers meet aliens?

Maybe! If they do, each craft has a 'golden record' with information for any intelligent aliens, including sounds and photos of Earth.

Voyager 1

Where is Voyager 1 going?

Just to 'outer space'! In a billion years it could be about halfway across our galaxy. It will keep going until something destroys it, which could be millions, perhaps billions, of years in the future.

I'm around 20 billion kilometres from Earth! I travel at about 60,000 kilometres an hour and can cover half a billion kilometres per year.

New Horizons

Arrokoth

Which spacecraft has visited the most distant object?

NASA's New Horizons probe flew close to an asteroid in the Kuiper Belt, called Arrokoth, in 2019. It took 9.5 years to get to Pluto, and another 3.5 years to reach Arrokoth.

Did you know?

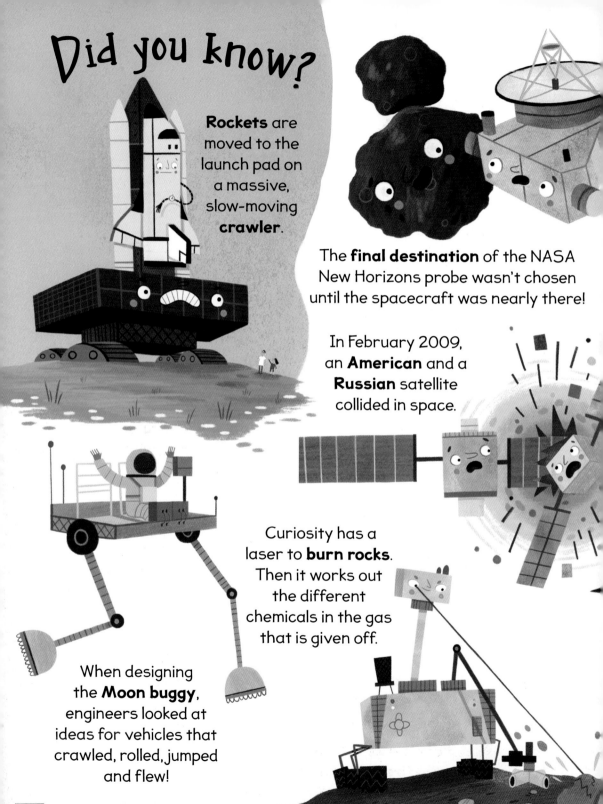

Rockets are moved to the launch pad on a massive, slow-moving **crawler**.

The **final destination** of the NASA New Horizons probe wasn't chosen until the spacecraft was nearly there!

In February 2009, an **American** and a **Russian** satellite collided in space.

Curiosity has a laser to **burn rocks**. Then it works out the different chemicals in the gas that is given off.

When designing the **Moon buggy**, engineers looked at ideas for vehicles that crawled, rolled, jumped and flew!

The Japanese spacecraft IKAROS is the first to use a **solar sail**.

The **computer** used to land on the Moon was less powerful than a modern **smartphone**.

Nooooooo!

The probe Cassini **plunged into Saturn** to avoid colliding with any moons.

There is a **Tesla car** in orbit around Earth.

The Chinese Chang'e 4 lander and rover Yutu were the **first to land** on the far side of the Moon, in 2019.

Lunar space station

There are plans for a base that will orbit near the Moon to support trips to the Moon, Mars and beyond.

What does the future look like?

There will be lots more satellites, many of them tiny, but also more space stations and telescopes.

I am going to investigate whether Titan can support life!

Dragonfly mission

A planned mission to Titan, Saturn's largest moon, will send 'rotorcraft' to explore the surface.

Moons of Mars

The Japanese space agency, JAXA, is planning a mission to investigate Mars' moons Phobos and Deimos.

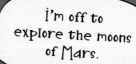

I'm off to explore the moons of Mars.

Mission to Mercury

The BepiColombo probe, launched by JAXA and ESA in 2018, will travel to Mercury, arriving in 2025.

Sail to the stars

We could see new kinds of sails that use solar wind, radiation or even just light to push spacecraft along.

I have been built to launch heavy objects into space!

Asteroid mines

Some organizations are hoping to trap asteroids and mine them for useful metals.

Mega rockets

New types of rocket to launch heavy objects are being developed, including NASA's SLS (super-heavy launch system).

A compendium of questions

Do probes ever come back?

The probe itself doesn't, but probes can return capsules. In 2006, the Stardust probe sent back dust from the comet Wild 2.

What does an astronaut wear under their EMU?

A giant nappy, and a body suit that has tubes to carry water and cool their body.

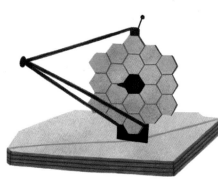

Are space shuttles still used?

No. The last space shuttle, Endeavour, made its final flight in 2011.

Why have a telescope in space?

It's free from distortion produced by Earth's atmosphere and it can also pick up ultraviolet radiation blocked by Earth's atmosphere.

How do astronauts talk to each other in space?

They have a radio link, with microphones in their helmets.

Where are you going?

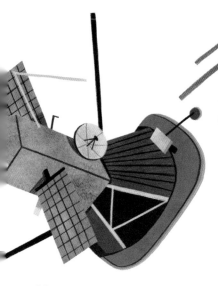

What is the fastest spacecraft?

Juno reached 266,000 kilometres an hour in 2016. The Parker Solar Probe should manage 692,000 kilometres an hour in 2024.

Have we sent landers to Venus?

Yes, but they don't last long! They are quickly destroyed by the extreme heat and pressure of the planet's atmosphere at the surface.

How are things held down in the ISS?

Lots of things are held down with Velcro or magnets.

How do astronauts get food on the ISS?

It is sent with other supplies carried to and fro by Soyuz spacecraft.

Out on a spacewalk!

How does my BODY fight germs?

Answer on page 150

Why does A BALLOON go bang?

Answer on page 165

Do fish sink or FLOAT?

Answer on page 161

140

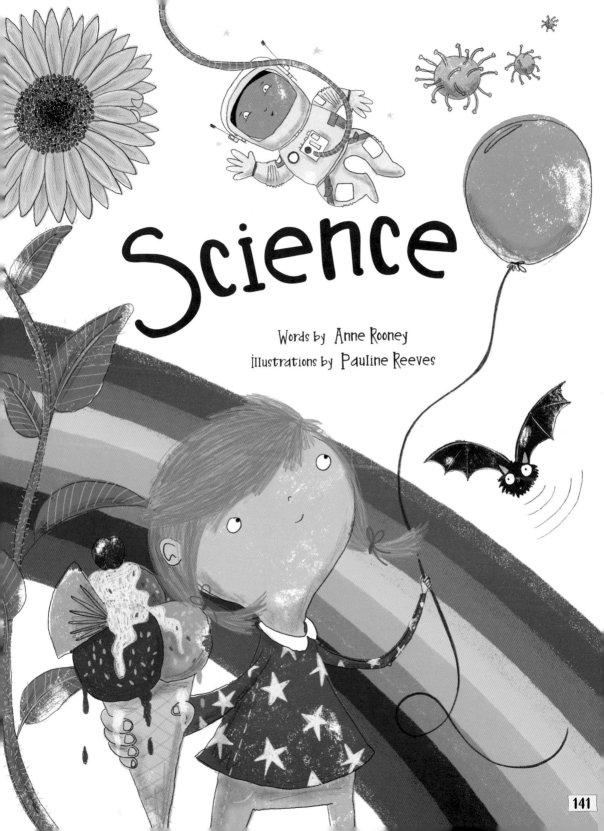

Science

Words by Anne Rooney

Illustrations by Pauline Reeves

How do we find things out?

We know about the world around us because scientists look carefully and carry out experiments. You could be a scientist! All you have to do is...

① Spot a problem

Keep your eyes and ears open. Look out for questions to ask and problems to solve.

② Have an idea

Think of something that could explain or solve the problem. This is your theory.

③ Design an experiment

Work out how to test your idea – an experiment. Change just one thing at a time to make a fair test.

④ Check what happens

Were you right? If not, you might need a new theory and a new experiment.

① Long ago, sailors were often ill with a disease called scurvy.

These long journeys are killing me! Can't somebody do something?

② Scientist James Lind (1716–1794) decided to investigate.

I think it might be what you're eating – or what you're not eating.

③

Cider

Oranges and lemons

Sea water

It's worth a try...

Vinegar

Lind chose six pairs of sick sailors. All had the same food, except he gave each pair one extra thing.

④

Months later, the sailors who had oranges and lemons were better. The rest were even more sick.

I want what he had!

Why do we need scientists?

The work of scientists can make life better. A discovery can lead to more questions and experiments. Science keeps on going.

Modern scientists found out that it is the Vitamin C in fruit that stops scurvy.

How many?

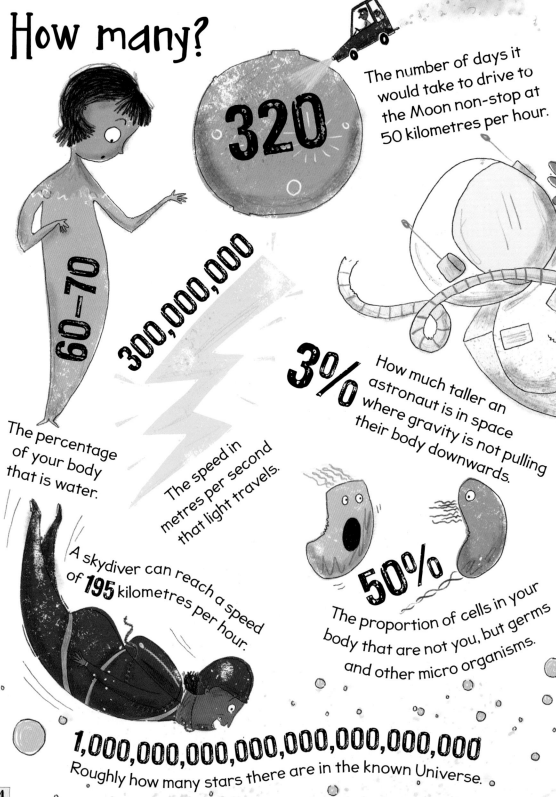

320

The number of days it would take to drive to the Moon non-stop at 50 kilometres per hour.

60-70

The percentage of your body that is water.

300,000,000

The speed in metres per second that light travels.

3%

How much taller an astronaut is in space where gravity is not pulling their body downwards.

50%

The proportion of cells in your body that are not you, but germs and other micro organisms.

A skydiver can reach a speed of **195** kilometres per hour.

1,000,000,000,000,000,000,000,000

Roughly how many stars there are in the known Universe.

80,000

The age in years of the oldest group of trees that share a single root system.

Our eyes can tell **10 million** different colours apart.

The cracks in breaking glass travel at **4830** kilometres per hour.

If all your blood vessels were laid end to end, they would stretch for **96,500** kilometres.

1,500,000,000,000,000,000

Roughly how many grains of sand there are on Earth.

340

The speed in metres per second that sound travels in air – a thunderclap one kilometre away would take 3 seconds to reach you.

What can you hear in space?

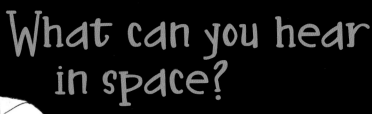

Nothing, there are no sounds in space. Sound travels as vibrations through matter. As space is empty, there is nothing for sound to travel through.

> I can hear noises inside my suit and in my headset but not from outside. Anything could sneak up on me!

> Dolphins can hear much higher sounds than humans!

Why do things sound different underwater?

The vibrations are going through water, not air, making things sound a bit different. We can hear higher sounds in water than in air.

> Dolphins use sound to hunt for food and find their way underwater. They make noises such as clicks and buzzes.

Do we all hear the same sounds?

No — children can hear higher and lower sounds than grown-ups. You can probably hear bats squeaking and high-pitched dog whistles, when older people hear nothing.

Can you hear the bats?

Can you hear the people?

Sri Lanka

Indian Ocean

East Africa

Krakatau

New Guinea

Australia

The eruption was so loud, it could be heard in all these places!

What's the loudest sound ever?

A volcano called Krakatau erupted in Indonesia in 1883, making the loudest sound humans have ever heard. It could be heard 5000 kilometres away.

How does electricity get to my house?

Electricity is a type of energy. It is generated in power stations then carried along a network of cables, all the way to the wires and power points throughout your house.

Can you spot some other objects that need electricity to work?

Lots of things we use every day, such as lights and computers, are powered by electricity. It makes the fridge cold, and the heater hot!

How is electricity made?

We get electricity by changing other forms of energy such as sunlight, wind, moving water, or by burning coal, oil or gas.

Coal, oil and gas are known as fossil fuels, because they come from the remains of animals and plants that lived long ago. A lot of our energy comes from burning fossil fuels.

Wires inside the walls carry electricity to all the places it's needed. We plug electrical objects into sockets in the wall.

Fossil fuels will run out in the future, and burning them causes pollution. So people are trying to use more energy from sources that can't be used up.

Solar power

Energy from sunlight is captured in solar panels and changed into electricity.

Water power

The energy of water held by a dam is changed into electrical energy.

Wind power

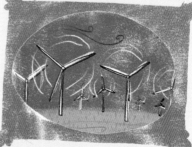

Wind turbines change the wind's movement energy into electricity.

Why do I feel ill?

Many illnesses are caused by germs – tiny things too small to see. There are germs everywhere. Your body tries to keep them out, and is good at fighting them when they get in.

How does my body fight germs?

It makes special cells (tiny parts of your body) that attack germs and anything else that shouldn't be inside you.

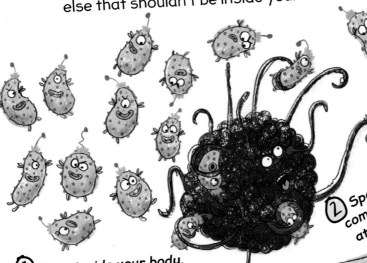

③ They destroy the germs by swallowing them whole!

② Special body cells come to the rescue by attacking the germs.

① Once inside your body, germs set up home and start reproducing – soon there are lots and lots.

What is a fever?

You might feel hot when you're ill. Your body pushes its temperature up to kill off germs that don't like the heat. This doesn't feel good, but it does you good!

Can I get the same type of germ again?

When you catch an illness like chickenpox, your body learns how to fight it. You probably won't get it again: if another chickenpox germ comes along, your body can deal with it quickly — it doesn't stand a chance.

While your body is fighting germs, you might feel ill. You might be sick, feel too hot, cough, sneeze or have aches and pains.

Did you know?

There are **meteorites** — tiny bits of rock from space — all around. One hits each square metre of ground about once a year.

Some **plants** eat insects and even small animals.

If you break a **magnet** in half, you get two magnets, each with a north and south pole.

If we could drill a hole right through the **Earth**, things wouldn't fall straight through; they would get to the middle and stop.

Bamboo grows so fast you can watch it get taller. It can grow 91 centimetres in a single day.

Nine tenths of an **iceberg** is under water. Ice only just floats, so not much sticks out.

If you put a **carnation** in coloured water, it will eventually suck up the water and turn the same colour.

If there was no air, a **feather** and **cricket ball** dropped from the same height would hit the ground together.

The **Apollo spacecraft** were landed on the Moon by a computer less powerful than a smartphone.

The largest land animal ever was **Patagotitan**, a dinosaur that weighed about 70 tonnes and was 37 metres long.

i weighed about the same as 12 African elephants!

Some **volcanic rocks** float on water. This is because they are full of air bubbles.

If you float a **needle** on water it lines up to point north/south.

Earth's continents move slowly all the time, so the **Atlantic Ocean** grows a few centimetres wider each year.

Why do I have a shadow?

Your body blocks light coming from the Sun or a lamp, making a darker patch on the other side.

Why is my reflection the wrong way round?

Light from the left side of your body travels to the mirror and bounces off, making the left side of your reflection.

If you were standing where your reflection is, that would be your right side, so it looks the wrong way round.

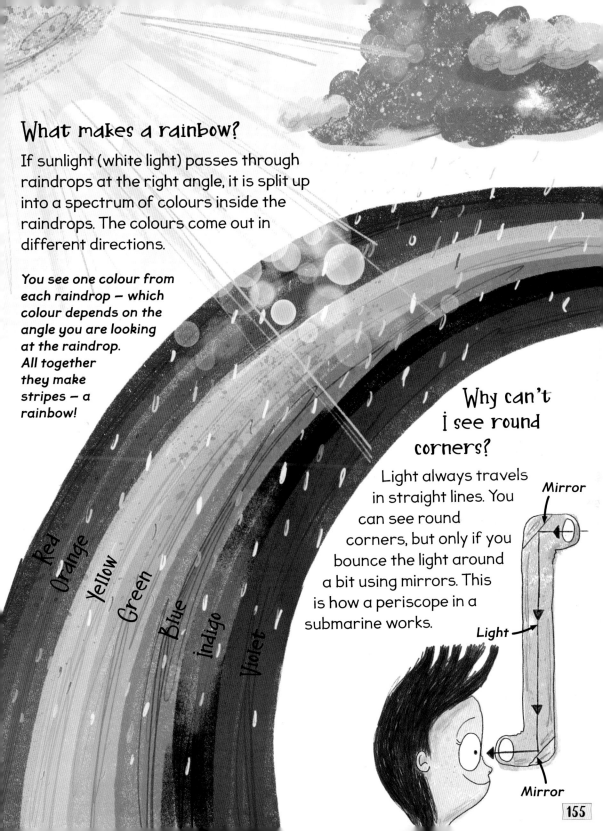

What makes a rainbow?

If sunlight (white light) passes through raindrops at the right angle, it is split up into a spectrum of colours inside the raindrops. The colours come out in different directions.

You see one colour from each raindrop — which colour depends on the angle you are looking at the raindrop. All together they make stripes — a rainbow!

Red
Orange
Yellow
Green
Blue
Indigo
Violet

Why can't I see round corners?

Light always travels in straight lines. You can see round corners, but only if you bounce the light around a bit using mirrors. This is how a periscope in a submarine works.

Mirror

Light

Mirror

Why do things fall?

The force of gravity pulls objects towards the centre of the Earth – downwards! Gravity is everywhere in the Universe, pulling things with less mass towards things with more mass. The Earth has more mass than anything on it.

Things only move if a force acts on them. You can think of forces as 'pushes' or 'pulls'. I'm falling because gravity is pulling me down.

Gravity →

← Drag

Why does a parachute slow your fall?

A force called drag acts on the parachute. When the parachute opens, air is trapped under it. The air has to be pushed out of the way for the parachute to fall. The air holds the parachute up while gravity pulls it down.

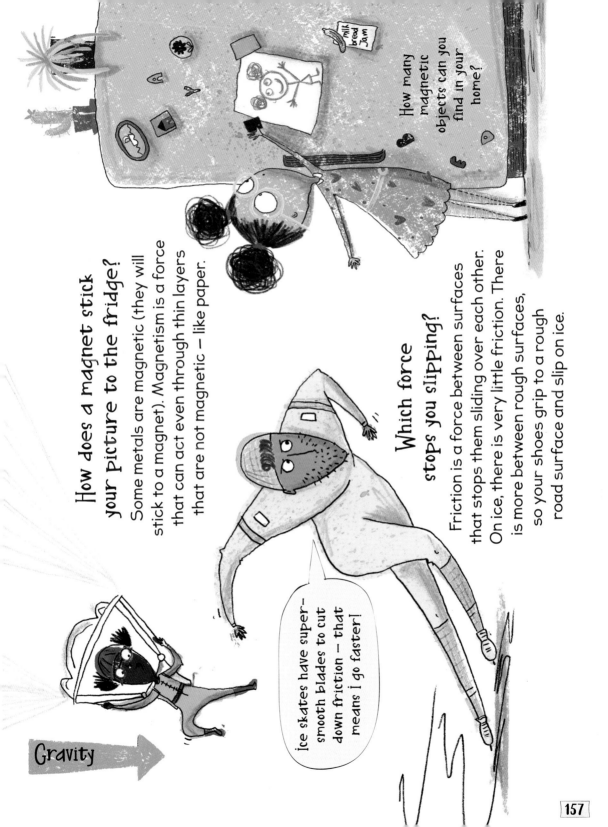

How does a magnet stick your picture to the fridge?

Some metals are magnetic (they will stick to a magnet). Magnetism is a force that can act even through thin layers that are not magnetic — like paper.

How many magnetic objects can you find in your home?

Which force stops you slipping?

Friction is a force between surfaces that stops them sliding over each other. On ice, there is very little friction. There is more between rough surfaces, so your shoes grip to a rough road surface and slip on ice.

Ice skates have super-smooth blades to cut down friction — that means I go faster!

Gravity

Would you rather?

Would you rather be a **vulture** that eats dead animals or a **worm** that eats soil?

If you were a superhero, would you rather have enough **friction** to walk up walls or be able to turn **gravity** off and float around?

Would it be better to be able to see **round corners** or in the **dark**?

Would you prefer to study **tigers** in the jungle or explore scary **volcanoes**?

Would you rather invent an amazing new **material** or design a fantastic **vehicle**?

Would you rather be **super-stretchy** like elastic, or **super-springy** and bounce everywhere?

Time for adventure! Would you rather be an **astronaut** going to Mars or a **diver** exploring the deepest oceans?

Would you rather be so **light** you can walk on water...

...or so **dense** you could walk along the seabed?

Gravity

A ship made of solid metal, without any air in it, would sink.

Which force pushes up?

Buoyancy

Buoyancy! Buoyancy is a force that pushes upwards through a fluid (such as water or air) against the weight of an object. When the weight pushing down (gravity) and the buoyancy are equal, the object doesn't move up or down.

Why do ships float?

Whether something sinks or floats depends on its density (how heavy something is for its volume). Most big ships are made of metal. Metal is more dense than water, but a ship floats because it is mostly full of air.

If we put in so much stuff the ship becomes denser than water, it will sink.

Do fish sink or float?

They can do both! Fish are almost the same density as water. Many types have a swim bladder, which is a sac filled with gas in their stomach. The amount of gas controls the fish's buoyancy to keep it at the right level in the water. It can add more gas to go up, or lose gas to go down.

What is matter?

Matter is everything around you! It has three states: a solid, a liquid, or a gas.

Solid
A solid (like paper, wood or plastic) can hold its shape.

Liquid
A liquid can't hold its shape. It spreads out into a pool unless it's held in a container.

The gas in my balloon can't get out.

Gas
A gas doesn't hold its shape. It spreads out as far as possible. To keep a gas in one place, we put it in a closed container.

Why does ice cream melt?

Materials change state as they heat up or cool down. Heating a solid above its melting point turns it to liquid. The melting point for ice cream is 0° Celsius.

To keep ice cream frozen solid, we store it in the freezer.

How does a liquid become a gas?

Heating a liquid to its boiling point turns it to a gas. The boiling point of water is 100° Celsius.

Melting and boiling are reversible. If you cool a gas below its boiling point it becomes liquid again. And if you cool a liquid below its melting point it becomes solid.

Not all things melt when heated — some just burn. Which of these things do you think would melt?

- Woolly sweater
- Egg
- Glass bottle
- Sausage
- Toffee
- Metal key
- Book
- Wooden chair

Answer:
glass, toffee and metal melt

A compendium of questions

Why is it cold at the North and South Poles?

The Earth is like a ball, so the top and bottom don't get much direct sunlight as they face away from the Sun.

Where do stars go in the daytime?

Nowhere! The light from the Sun is so bright that they just don't show up in daytime.

Moon

Why does the tide go in and out?

The Moon's gravity pulls on the oceans. As the Earth turns, the water is pulled one way and then the other.

What is a cloud made of?

Tiny drops of water, so light that they are held up by the air. If too much water collects, the drops get heavier and fall as rain.

This way up!

Why do I burp?

Food breaking down in your stomach makes gases. This collects in bubbles which come out at your top or bottom!

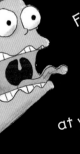

At the South Pole, which way is up?

Towards the sky. Down is always towards the centre of the Earth. There is no up or down in space.

Could astronauts go to the Sun?

No – the Sun is far too hot for any person or spaceship to survive getting close to.

Why does a balloon go bang?

The air inside is under a lot of pressure. When the balloon bursts, air rushes out in a fast-moving wave. We hear this as a bang.

Why isn't the world covered in poo?

Poo is eaten and broken down by dung beetles, worms and micro organisms. So poo is food for some things!

Why don't I freeze solid in icy weather?

You're warm-blooded, which means your body uses energy to keep you at a safe temperature.

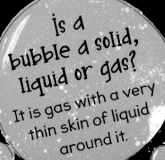

Is a bubble a solid, liquid or gas?

It is gas with a very thin skin of liquid around it.

Can I be a scientist when I grow up?

Yes! Anyone can be a scientist — just stay curious!

What is MY SKELETON made of?

Answer on page 176

How DO i REMEMBER things?

Answer on page 185

Why are CELLS so SPECIAL?

Answer on page 168

My Body

Words by Anne Rooney
Consulted by Kristina Routh
Illustrations by Ana Gomez

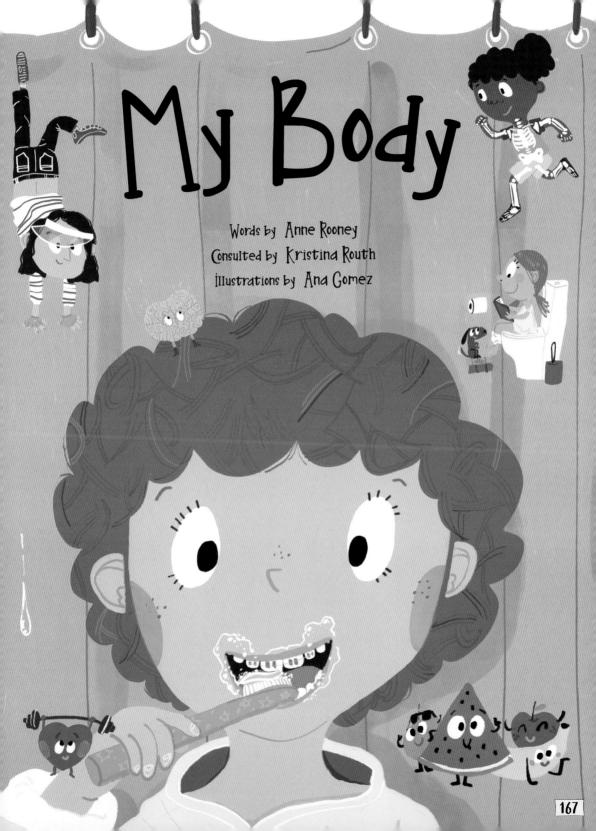

What is my body for?

Your body lets you see, hear, smell, taste and touch the world around you. You can use it to run, jump, think, talk, and have all kinds of fun. Without it, you couldn't do anything.

> Our bodies look different on the outside, but inside we all have bones, muscles and blood.

> Cells make up tissue such as bone, muscle and blood.

Why are cells so special?

Because they are the tiny building blocks that together make up your body. Different cells do different jobs. You have blood cells, bone cells, skin cells and lots more.

Bone cells make up your skeleton

168

X-rays can check for broken bones.

How can doctors see inside our bodies?

Doctors can look inside the body with scans and X-rays to see where all the parts are and how they fit together. They can even look at single cells with microscopes that magnify them.

Muscle cells help to form every muscle in your body

Your blood contains trillions of red blood cells

Why do I need to eat?

Food provides the energy your body needs to keep working. Chemicals from food repair your body and help it grow. Your body breaks down food and rearranges the chemicals to make skin, hair, bones and all the other parts.

Fruit and vegetables
Eat lots of these for fibre and goodness

Can I balance my food?

Yes you can, but not on your head! It's important to eat a wide range of foods from different food groups to make sure you stay fit and healthy.

Protein
Meat, fish and beans help your body grow and repair itself

Sugar and fats give you energy, but eating too much of them can be unhealthy.

Fats and sugars
Foods high in fats and sugars should only be eaten in small amounts

Carbohydrates
Bread, potatoes, rice and pasta give you lots of energy

Dairy
Milk, cheese and yoghurt keep your bones and teeth strong

Drink lots of water!

Eat five portions of fruit and vegetables every day.

Why is water so important?
About 60 percent of your body is water — it's in every cell. But you lose water when you pee and sweat, and every time you breathe out. You need to drink to replace the water you lose.

What happens when I eat?

The food you eat takes a long and twisty route through your digestive system. At each stage, your body pulls out the good things it needs.

Always wash your hands before eating.

① How do teeth help?

Your teeth break up food as you chew. They chew it into smaller pieces and mash it around. Food mixes with saliva in your mouth, making it easier to swallow.

② Where does food go first?

When you swallow, food goes into a tube in your throat called your oesophagus (say 'ee-sof-a-guss'). Muscles push the food down to your stomach, squeezing behind the lump of food so that it moves along.

Oesophagus

From mouth to stomach takes 5–8 seconds

③ Why is there acid in my stomach?

Acid dissolves food into a gloopy liquid. Muscles in your stomach also churn the mixture around to break it up.

④ What goes on in my intestines?

A milky mushy liquid moves into and through your intestines where nutrients (useful chemicals) and water are absorbed. The leftover parts are turned into... poo!

⑤ Why do i need to poo?

To get rid of the bits that your body doesn't need. These parts are squashed together and mixed with dead cells and water from your gut. They leave your body when you go to the toilet.

Always wash your hands after going to the toilet.

We're going down! Weee!

③

Food stays in your stomach for 2–6 hours. It turns to a milky mush called chyme (say 'kime')

Stomach
GLOOP!

④

Large intestine

Small intestine

POO!

⑤

The journey through your intestines can take 12–18 hours

173

How many?

35 The number of tonnes of food the average person eats in their life.

110,000 The number of hairs on the head of a dark-haired person; blondes have more and redheads have fewer.

37 trillion The number of human cells in an adult body.

1.5–2 The area in square metres of an adult's skin.

0.5 The volume of gas in litres that your gut produces each day.

Your nose can detect **1 trillion** smells.

69 The largest number of babies anyone has had.

16 The speed in kilometres per hour of a sneeze.

A hair grows **1.25** centimetres each month.

900 The length in centimetres of the longest-ever fingernail.

120 The speed in metres per second of a message travelling along a nerve.

5 The amount in litres of blood in an average adult human.

3 The length in millimetres of your smallest bone (it's inside your ear).

What is my skeleton made of?

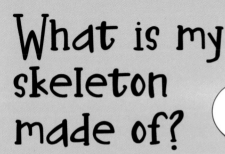

Imagine how floppy and blobby you'd be without bones!

Bones form the rigid framework for your body — your skeleton. They support your body and provide somewhere for your muscles to fix to.

Skull

Clavicle

Jaw

Humerus

Ribs

Ulna

Sternum

Radius

Pelvis

Spine

How do muscles move me?

Most muscles are fixed to your bones. As they contract, they pull the bones along with them, moving your body. Being active makes your muscles strong. Run, swim, jump, cycle — do anything you like!

Femur

Patella

Biceps muscle contracts to bend your arm

contract

relax

Fibula

Tibia

Tendon attaches muscle to bone

Phalanges

Triceps muscle relaxes

Which muscle works the hardest?

Your heart works harder than any other muscle. It never stops pumping blood around your body throughout your life.

i need exercise too! it helps to make me strong.

Activities like dancing are good for getting your heart working.

Knee joint

Ankle joint

Hip joint

Joints make you flexible, you couldn't move without them.

Elbow joint

Wrist joint

How does my body bend?

You have lots of joints in your body such as in your knees, elbows, shoulders, ankles and wrists. These are places where bones meet, and they allow your body to bend or move in different ways.

Activities like swimming make you breathe fast

Lung

Heart

Lung

What happens when I breathe?

When you breathe in, your lungs fill with air. Oxygen from the air goes into your blood and is delivered to your whole body. Old air is pushed out when you breathe out.

How does my blood deliver oxygen?

Your blood flows through tubes called blood vessels. These reach every single part of your body to make sure you have all the oxygen you need. Your heart and blood together are called the circulatory system.

Blood vessels

Why does my heart thump?

When you exercise, your heart beats faster to pump blood around your body quickly, to deliver the oxygen your muscles need. You also breathe faster to get more oxygen, and you feel out of breath.

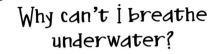

Why can't I breathe underwater?

Because you don't have gills like a fish! Your lungs can only take oxygen from the air. A fish's gills can take dissolved oxygen from water. When you swim underwater, you need to come to the surface for air.

Why am I ticklish?

Because you have a sense of touch! Your body uses five senses to find out about the world around you. Your senses pick up information and send it to your brain.

Cells in your nose help you recognize smells

Smell

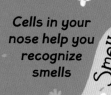

Eyes let in light to help you see all around you

See

Ears pick up sound vibrations to help you hear

Hear

Special areas on your tongue tell you what something tastes like

Touch

Skin is packed with touch sensors to help you feel

Taste

Why can't I see in the dark?

Because you need light to bounce off objects and into your eyes. A lens in your eye helps focus the light, and a nerve carries information to your brain to make an image — and that is what you see.

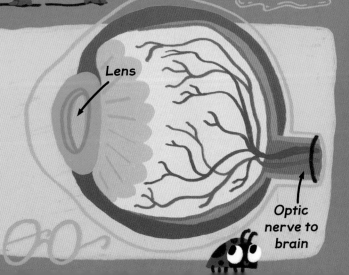

Lens

Optic nerve to brain

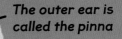

The outer ear is called the pinna

Why are ears a funny shape?

The shape of your ears helps to funnel sound into them. Sound is then carried inside your ear, where signals are sent along a nerve to your brain, so it can make sense of what you hear.

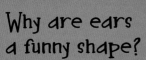

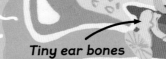

Soundwaves in

Tiny ear bones

Auditory nerve to brain

How do I smell?

Your sense of smell is produced by cells high above and behind your nose. Tiny particles of the thing you are smelling reach those cells.

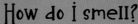

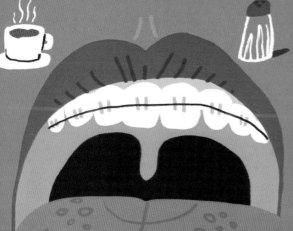

What helps me taste food?

Your tongue is covered with blobs surrounded by tiny taste buds. The taste buds send messages to your brain about the chemicals dissolved in food, and your brain turns the information into tastes.

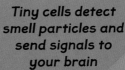

Tiny cells detect smell particles and send signals to your brain

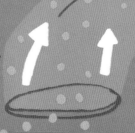

Smell particles go up your nose

Did you know?

Your **teeth** are as strong as a **shark's** teeth — but your jaws are smaller so you can't bite like a shark.

Babies can hear before they're born, though sounds from the outside are a bit **muffled**.

I hope I grow up to be a better singer than Mum.

An **adult** can survive three weeks without **food**, but only about four days without **water**.

Your **ears** are important to your sense of **balance**.

In **complete darkness,** your eyes could spot the light from a candle 48 kilometres away.

Some parts of your body are never replaced. The **enamel** on your teeth and the **goo** inside your **eyes** have to last a lifetime.

By the time you were six months old, your **eyes** were already **two thirds** their adult size.

Children can hear higher sounds than adults, including **bats** squeaking and **ultrasonic** dog whistles.

Fingerprints are not the body's only unique pattern. You can also be identified by your **tongue print**, your personal **smell** and the pattern in your **iris** (the coloured part of your eye).

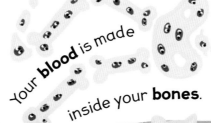

Your **blood** is made inside your **bones**.

Is my brain in charge?

What you say, think and how you move, and everything else you do, is controlled by your brain.

It receives information

A network of nerves tells your brain what is happening to your body. Your brain is linked to your body by your spinal cord

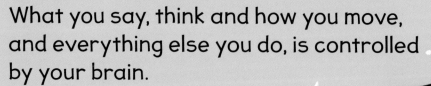

Stand on one foot and spin the ball.

Brain

Spinal cord

It sends messages

Your brain sends messages to your body, telling it how to react or move

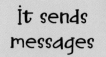

Nerve network

What do my nerves do?

Nerves are collections of nerve cells (neurons). They carry information between all parts of your body and brain. When you see, smell, taste or hear anything, information is carried by nerves to your brain super-quickly.

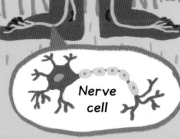

Nerve cell

5

Your brain is protected by your skull, and a layer of fluid

Think and plan

Touch and taste

Talk and smell

Hear

See

Move

Different areas of your brain control different things

How do I remember things?

Everything is stored in your brain, including memories, dreams and what you've learnt at school. Your brain stores some information for just seconds, and some for a lifetime.

④

Why do we say 'ouch'?

If you touch something hot, nerves carry signals to your spinal cord (1). This responds immediately (2) and sends a message through other nerves to make your hand move away (3). A slower message goes to your brain (4) that makes you feel pain and say 'ouch'.

①

Spinal cord

②

③

Why do I sleep?

Your body uses the time you're asleep to repair any injuries, grow, rest and sort out what you've experienced and learnt during the day. No one knows exactly how sleep works, but we do know that we can't live without it.

Does everyone dream?

Yes, but not everyone remembers their dreams. Most people have 3–5 dreams each night. Even cats and dogs have dreams!

No one knows what animals dream about!

Why are dreams so weird?

As your brain sorts through information while you sleep, it's in a jumbled order, with recent events mixed up with old memories. Some people think secret meanings are hidden in dreams.

Each dream can last 20 minutes or a few seconds

How much sleep do I need?

We need different amounts of sleep at different ages. Newborn babies sleep for a long time every day. Adults sleep less.

Hours

18
16
14
12
10
8
6
4
2
0

| Newborn | Pre-school | School | Teen | Adult |

Would you rather?

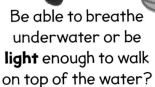

Be able to breathe underwater or be **light** enough to walk on top of the water?

Have a really long **tongue** or really long **fingers**?

Have **super-keen sight** or be able to hear very **quiet sounds** like ants munching their food?

Grow really long **fingernails** or really **long hair**?

Have **unbreakable** bones or **uncuttable** skin?

Have **wings** or a **tail**?

Be **wobbly** like a jellyfish with no bones, or have a **hard** outer shell like a tortoise?

Be entirely **furry** or entirely **bald**?

Have eyes in the back of your **head** or in the tips of your **fingers**?

Be able to run really **fast** or for a really **long** time?

189

Where do babies come from?

Babies come from inside their mum's body. A baby grows in the mum's uterus, where it gets everything it needs until it's ready to be born.

I can feel the baby kicking!

Goodness from the mother's food is carried along the cord to the baby

Egg cell divides again and again

Cord

Uterus

How fast does a baby grow?

Inside its mum, a baby grows really fast. It starts off as a tiny egg, which divides to make the billions of cells that make up the whole baby. After nine months, the baby is big enough to be born.

Day 1

Day 2

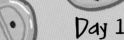

Days 3–4

12 weeks
5 centimetres

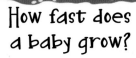

20 weeks
16 centimetres

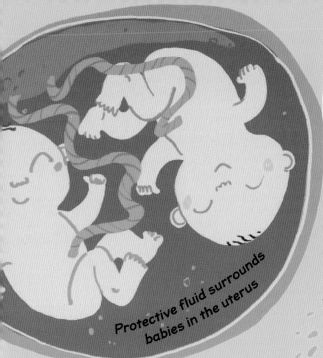

Protective fluid surrounds babies in the uterus

Can there be more than one baby?

If two eggs grow, or if one egg splits in half, there can be two babies — twins. Twins from two eggs look different, but twins from the same egg are identical.

WAAAH! WAAH!

32 weeks
42 centimetres

40 weeks
51 centimetres

Why do babies cry?

When babies are born, they can't talk or do anything for themselves. They cry to tell their parents that they're hungry, or they're cold — or that their nappy needs changing!

Am i always growing?

You keep growing from when you are born until your late teens or early twenties. But the speed you grow at slows down. A baby triples its weight in a year.

> Do you know how tall you are?

> Babies double their weight in five months. If you kept doing that you'd be huge!

5 years

6 months

10 years

Newborn

How do i get taller?

A soft, flexible substance called cartilage grows inside your bones, making them longer. The cartilage slowly hardens into bone.

Cartilage hardens to bone

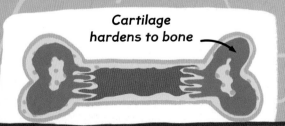

Why does my hair need cutting?

Your hair grows throughout your life, so you have to keep cutting it. Hair grows from a little pit on your scalp called a hair follicle, but the hair you can see is actually dead. That's why it doesn't hurt to have a haircut.

Hair follicle

Your ears keep getting bigger too, but very slowly.

15 years

20 years

70 years

Grandma? Grandpa?

Do we shrink as we get older?

Yes! The bones of the spine get squashed closer together over the years. Some older people also get a curved spine and stoop, and that makes them look even shorter.

A compendium of questions

Why do my first teeth fall out?

Your first teeth are temporary — you have them until your mouth grows large enough for your permanent teeth. You have 20 first teeth, and they are replaced by larger, stronger, teeth.

What are hiccups?

If the muscle across your chest suddenly squeezes, it can snap shut the opening to your vocal flaps, making the 'hic' sound.

Why do we like sugar if it's bad for us?

Millions of years ago, our ancestors ate a sugar-rich fruit diet. So gradually people grew to like sweet things.

Why do i yawn?

No one's quite sure, but possibly as a way of getting more oxygen into your body quickly.

What are goosebumps?

They are bumps on your skin where tiny muscles make your hairs stand up if you are cold or scared.

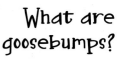

Why do we get wrinkles?

As skin ages, it loses its elasticity, so it can't spring back into shape after stretching (such as when you smile).

Why don't I have to remember to breathe?

Your brain deals with all kinds of automatic activities without you having to think about them, including breathing, and digesting food.

What is my tummy button for?

When you were inside your mother, you got nutrients and oxygen through the umbilical cord that connected you to her body. The tummy button is what's left after the cord is cut.

Why is blood red?

Blood contains a chemical for carrying oxygen that contains iron. When this chemical picks up oxygen, it turns redder.

What makes a scab?

When your blood meets the air, special cells called platelets break up and mix with a protein in blood to make tangly fibres, forming a scab.

Why do I sleep more when I'm ill?

Your body needs energy to fight the illness, so to save energy it makes you sleep.

Who LiKES eating greens?

Answer on page 201

What makes flamingos PINK?

Answer on page 200

Answer on page 200

Why do CROCODILES eat stones?

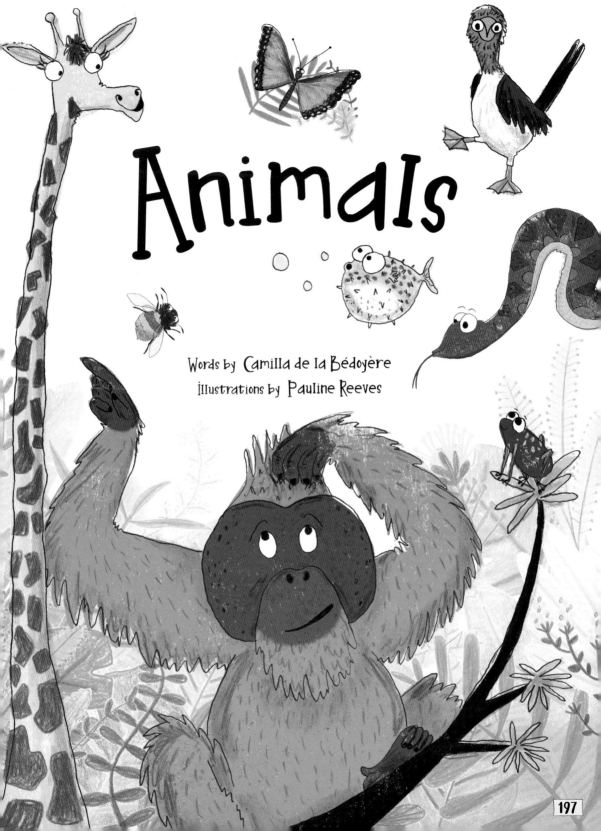

Animals

Words by Camilla de la Bédoyère

Illustrations by Pauline Reeves

What is an animal?

Animals are living things that do all of these things...

① Have babies

All animals can make new life like themselves — this is called **having babies**, or **reproduction**.

② Breathe

Animals **breathe** to take air into their bodies. The body needs a gas in the air called oxygen to keep working.

③ Use senses

An animal uses the **senses** of touch, taste, smell, sight and hearing to find out what is going on around it.

Those leaves look tasty!

④ Move

Most animals **move** to get to food and water, to find safe places, and to escape from danger.

I learnt to stand up 30 minutes after I was born. How old were you when you learnt to stand?

⑤ Eat

Animals must **eat** food to stay alive. Food gives them energy so they can **move** and **grow**.

Munch!

⑥ Get rid of waste

Waste is leftover food that an animal's body doesn't need.

Waste not want not! Dung beetles like me use elephant poo for lots of things!

⑦ Grow

All animals start small and **grow** bigger until they are old enough to **have babies** of their own.

Why do crocodiles eat stones?

Because they swallow their meaty meals whole, and the stones help to grind up the food in their tummies!

Crocs are one of the world's biggest carnivores, or meat-eaters. We eat fish, birds, rats, snakes, lizards and even deer and pigs.

What makes flamingos pink?

Flamingos are pink because they eat pink shrimps that live in VERY salty lakes! They feed with their heads upside down.

Can you see any other upside-down eaters around here?

Who likes eating greens?

Leaves and other greens taste great to herbivores (plant-eaters) like sloths. Some greens are tough to eat, so they spend lots of time chewing.

Anteaters like me eat ants and termites – thousands of them every day! We lick them up with our long, sticky tongues.

Are animals picky eaters?

They can be! Some only eat one special food. Others, like tiger sharks and brown bears, will eat almost anything they can find!

What are senses?

Senses are the body's way of finding out about the world. Animals use senses to locate food, find their way about, avoid danger and make friends. The five main senses are **hearing**, **sight**, **smell**, **taste** and **touch**.

HEARING

Ear

Do bugs have ears?

Yes – lots of bugs can hear better than humans, but our ears can be in strange places! I'm a bush cricket, and my ears are on my legs.

What are whiskers for?

TOUCH

A cat's whiskers are super-sensitive. I use them to feel things – they can tell me if a space I want to crawl into is too small for my body.

How do snakes smell?

Snakes can smell with their tongues. They flick them in the air to detect any appealing pongs!

SMELL

TASTE

Why is it a bad idea to lick a frog?

I make a foul-tasting slime in my skin. It stops animals from eating me.

SIGHT

Do all animals have two eyes?

Some animals have more than two! Most spiders have eight eyes but cave spiders have none. They live in caves where it's always dark.

Did you know?

A **fulmar** is a foul seabird. It spits a stinky oil at anyone who gets too close.

The **giraffe** is the tallest animal that lives on land.

Lobsters have blue blood and some dogs have blue tongues.

When a **sandtiger shark** wants to sink to the seabed, it has to burp first!

A spiny **sea urchin** is covered in tiny feet. Its mouth is on its bottom!

Mimic octopuses can change shape and colour. They can pretend to be fish or sea snakes.

Sweat bees like the smell and taste of human sweat!

If a **sponge** is broken into bits, this strange sea creature is able to put itself back together again.

The **dung beetle** is the strongest animal on Earth. If it were the size of a human it could pull six buses full of people!

A **spider** eats about 2000 bugs a year.

Australian **burrowing frogs** cover themselves in slime, so when flies land on them they get stuck — and the frogs can gobble them up.

Bees waggle their bottoms in a crazy dance to tell each other where to find the best flowers.

Hippos don't just yawn when they are tired — they also yawn when they are angry or scared.

A **blue whale** eats millions of pink shrimps, so its poo is pink too. Each poo can be bigger than you!

A **catfish** can use its whole body to taste. Its skin is covered with taste buds.

What's inside an animal?

If you had to build an animal from scratch, here's what you would need...

Spine

Ribs

① Framework

Most big animals have a **skeleton** – a framework of bones beneath their skin. Smaller animals have a tough outside – like a shell or strong skin – called an **exoskeleton**.

③ Inner workings

Soft, squishy body parts called organs do useful jobs such as thinking, breathing and turning food into energy.

Brain

Tail

Lung

Liver

Heart

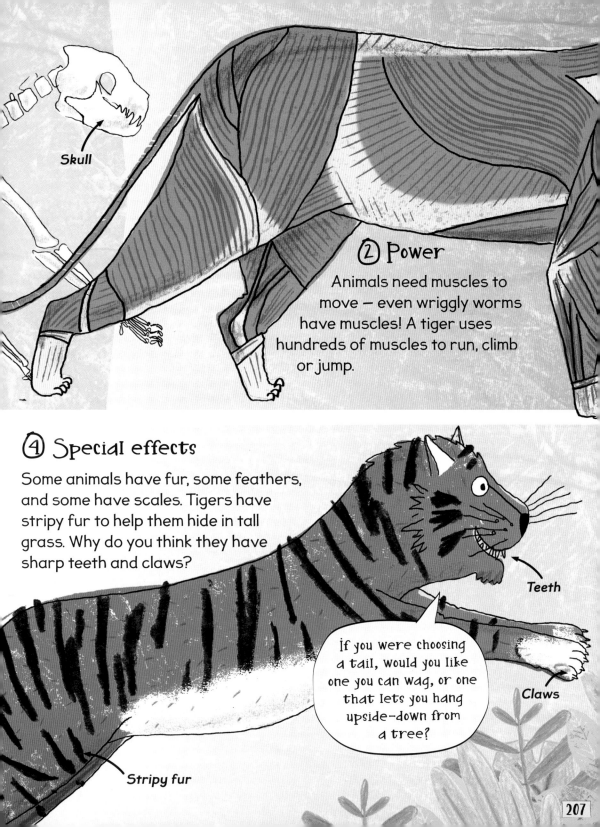

Skull

② Power

Animals need muscles to move — even wriggly worms have muscles! A tiger uses hundreds of muscles to run, climb or jump.

④ Special effects

Some animals have fur, some feathers, and some have scales. Tigers have stripy fur to help them hide in tall grass. Why do you think they have sharp teeth and claws?

If you were choosing a tail, would you like one you can wag, or one that lets you hang upside-down from a tree?

Teeth

Claws

Stripy fur

Why are you blue?

Colours and patterns make an animal beautiful! They can also make an animal look scary, or help it to hide.

Blue-ringed octopus

My colour is a sign of danger. When i'm scared, blue circles appear on my skin. They are a warning that i can kill any attackers with venom.

Blue morpho butterfly

Danger or disguise?

Some animals blend into the background. This is called camouflage. Others have colours and patterns that warn enemies to stay away. Which of these creatures are using camouflage, and which are using warning colours?

Strawberry poison dart frog

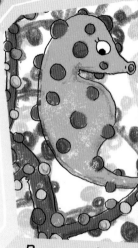

Pygmy seahorse

Blue shark

My colours help me hide. A blue or dark grey shark can prowl through the sea, unseen by the fish it is looking for.

Would you rather have blue feet, like me, or a blue bum, like a baboon?

Blue-footed booby

Southern crowned-pigeon

My beautiful blue feathers make me look healthy and fit to attract a mate.

Leaf insect

Banded sea krait

Lion

Would you rather?

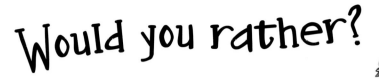

Winter is coming! Would you prefer to travel to somewhere warm, like a **sand martin**, or curl up and sleep through it, like a **dormouse**?

Zzzzz...

Would you rather be spotted like a **leopard**, or striped like a **tiger**?

Is it better to have a long neck, like a **giraffe**...

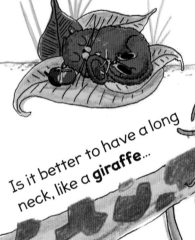

...or lots of arms like an **octopus**?

You look soooo cute!

A giraffe uses its long neck to reach leaves in tall trees. An octopus uses its arms to move, touch, taste and gather food.

If you were an animal baby would you prefer to sit in dad's pouch, like a **seahorse**, or in mum's, like a **kangaroo**?

It's picnic time! Would you prefer to tuck into a rotting dead animal like a **vulture**, or suck down some animal poo like a **sea cucumber**?

Erm... yummy?

Would you rather have armour like a **pangolin**, or spikes like a **pufferfish**?

WHOOSH!

Would you rather be able to dive through the air at 200 kilometres an hour like a **peregrine falcon**, or fly 15,000 kilometres in a single journey like an **albatross**?

Is it better to be best friends with a **shark** or a **crocodile**?

Sharks and crocodiles are both big carnivores. That means they eat other animals, so it's probably not a good idea to try to make friends with either!

Will you play with me?

Why do spiders do cartwheels?

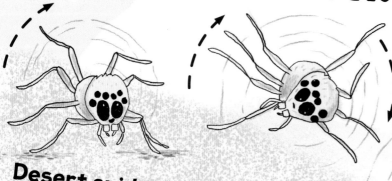

TUMBLE

Desert spiders that have to get across hot sand do cartwheels so their feet don't get burnt!

How high can you jump?

BOUNCE

LEAP

Kangaroos can jump up to 3 metres into the air, but we can't walk, or move backwards.

Why do orangutans have long arms?

Long arms are great for swinging through trees. We also have hands for gripping branches and grabbing fruit.

SWING

Antelopes leap several metres at a time, springing up in the air to escape from danger.

Which bird flies, but goes nowhere?

HOVER

A hummingbird does. It flaps and twists its wings so that it can hover in front of a flower, where it drinks the sweet nectar.

I can leap more than 100 times my own height.

SPRING

Fleas jump so they can leap from animal to animal, where they suck blood!

How fast do cheetahs sprint?

A cheetah is the fastest running animal on the planet. It can reach top speeds of up to 100 kilometres an hour.

① Built for speed

A cheetah's body is packed with small but powerful muscles.

Why do cheetahs run fast?

Like many hunters, cheetahs turn on the speed when they want to catch their lunch! The antelope they chase need to be fast too, if they hope to escape.

Why are tortoises so slow?

Tortoises plod along slowly because they don't need speed to catch their lunch – they eat grass! They don't need to be fast to escape from danger either because their tough shells protect them like a suit of armour.

② Big strides

It has a super-bendy
spine and long,
slim legs.

③ Long leap

All four of a cheetah's feet
leave the ground as it runs.

Why do crabs run sideways?

Because the way their legs bend
means they can't run forwards!

Who's playing statues?

During the day, a potoo
bird doesn't move at all! It
pretends to be a branch.
At night, it flies about,
hunting bugs to eat.

How many?

A squid has **2** tentacles...

... and it has **8** arms.

An octopus has **3** hearts but an earthworm has **5**.

Sea otters have **800 million** hairs on their bodies.

Tree kangaroos can jump **30** metres from a tree to the ground below.

A snow leopard can leap more than **10** metres in a single bound.

A snake can live for up to **6** months without eating.

A giraffe's tongue is **45** centimetres long.

20 The number of hours three-toed sloths, koalas and lions might sleep in one day.

500,000

The number of kilometres a sooty tern can fly without stopping for a rest.

Monarch butterflies can go on incredible journeys — one butterfly flew more than **4000** kilometres to lay its eggs!

4

The number of wings a bee has.

1

The number of hours it takes a snail to slime its way along just **1** metre of ground.

The largest number of legs ever counted on a millipede.

750

A mother cane toad can lay **35,000** eggs at a time.

The length, in centimetres, of the longest insect — a type of stick insect called Chan's megastick.

36

Is anyone at home?

Yes! An animal's home is a safe place where it can look after its babies. Animal homes are called habitats. They can be as big as an ocean or as small as a single leaf.

Froghopper nest

Who lives in a home made of spit?

Young froghopper insects build a home of froth around themselves! This 'spit' keeps them safe while they grow.

Why do frogs like water?

Because they need to lay their eggs in it. They are amphibians, which means they can live in water or on land.

Some animals that live in or near water have to come up to the surface to breathe air.

Others have gills and breathe underwater.

Frogs like to live in wet places

Can animals make things?

Yes, some animals are expert builders and can make super structures.

① *A hoop of grass...*

② *...turns into a ball...*

③ *...and then a home.*

Which bird builds the best nest?

A dad weaver bird makes his nest by stitching blades of grass together, then stuffing feathers inside to make a soft bed. He sings to tell mum she can lay her eggs there.

① *Strong silk makes the frame*

② *Sticky silk is used in the spiral*

Why do spiders build webs?

So they can trap flies. A spider makes the silk in its body and then spins it into a web.

Who loves mud?

Millions of termites do! They build their huge towering homes from mud. A group of termites that live together is called a colony, and their home can last for years.

There are passages, tunnels, and places to store food inside

A termite mound can be more than 2 metres high!

HOME SWEET HOME

A single queen lays all the eggs

What's the point of mums and dads?

Some animal babies look after themselves, but many need mums and dads to give them food and keep them safe.

Where do penguins keep their eggs?

Emperor penguins like us keep our eggs off the ice by holding them on our feet. The skin on our tummies is covered with fluffy feathers to keep our chicks warm.

How does a baby orca sleep?

Baby orcas can swim as soon as they are born, and they sleep while they are swimming! Orcas can rest one half of their brain at a time. The other half stays wide-awake.

A baby orca is called a calf

Do baby animals drink milk?

Yes, furry animals are called mammals and they feed their babies with milk. A polar bear mum looks after her cubs in a snowy den during the long, cold winter.

ZZZZZZ

Would you rather have an orca, a penguin or a polar bear for a parent?

A compendium of questions

Are sharks the most dangerous animals?

Sharks don't usually attack people. Snakes, donkeys and dogs hurt people more often than sharks!

Can a lizard run across water?

A basilisk lizard can. It runs really fast and uses its big feet and tail to help it balance on top of the water.

How does a squid escape from a hungry shark?

A squid squirts jets of water, and zooms off! The jets of water push the squid forward. This is called jet propulsion.

Why do jellyfish wobble?

Jellyfish don't have any bones and their bodies are full of water, like real jelly!

Do all animals have bones?

Mammals, birds, reptiles, amphibians and fish have bones. All other animals — including bugs, crabs and octopuses — don't.

What is venom?

Venom is a poison. Venomous animals can inject it using their fangs, claws, spines or stings. They use it to defend themselves, or to kill animals for food.

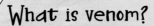

How do animals glide?

Gliding lizards, frogs and squirrels have large flaps of skin that they stretch out before they leap from a tree. The skin works like a parachute to help them glide, and land softly.

Is a bat a bird?

No, it's a flying mammal. Bats are the only mammals that fly.

Do camels keep water in their humps?

No – a camel's hump is full of fat, not water.

Do lions purr?

Big cats roar but can't purr, and small cats purr but can't roar. Big cats sometimes make a noise like a growly purr!

What's the smallest bird?

A bee hummingbird. It's smaller than your thumb. An ostrich is the biggest bird.

How many animals are in the world?

No one knows, but there are billions of ants, so it must be lots!

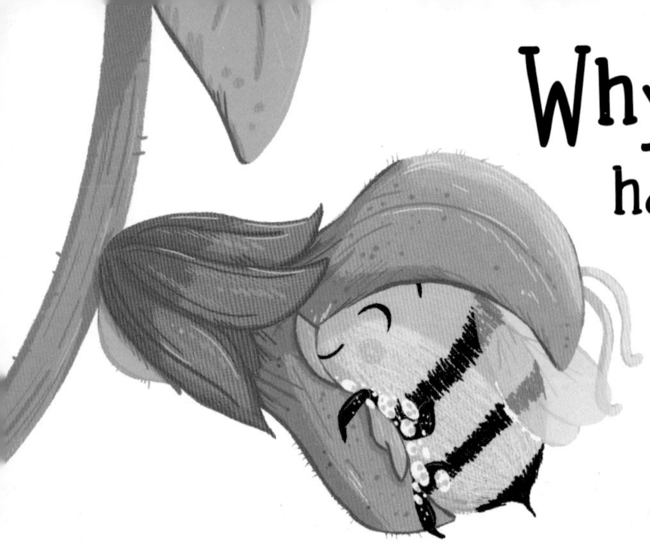

Why do BEES have BASKETS?

Answer on page 237

Which plant stinks of ROTTING socks?

Answer on page 249

Why do BANANAS need bats?

Answer on page 237

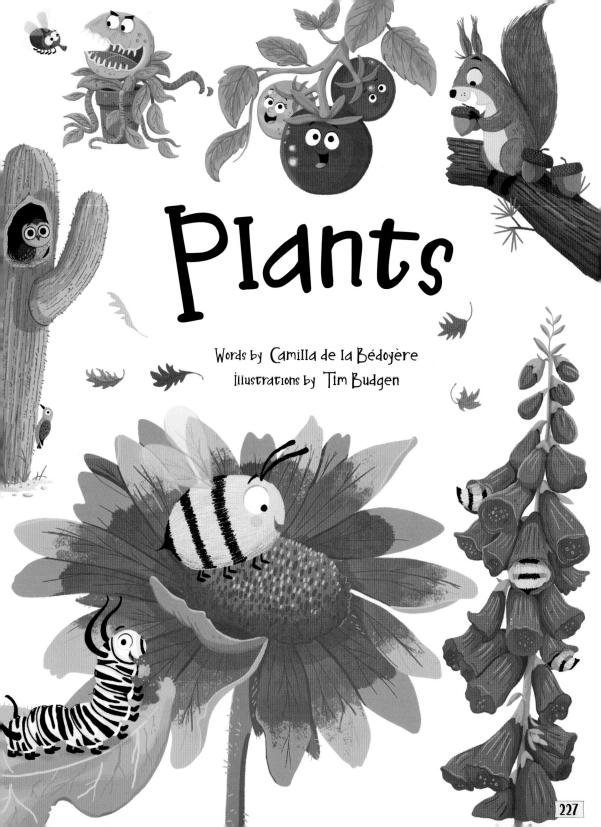

Plants

Words by Camilla de la Bédoyère

Illustrations by Tim Budgen

What is a plant?

Plants are living things that can...

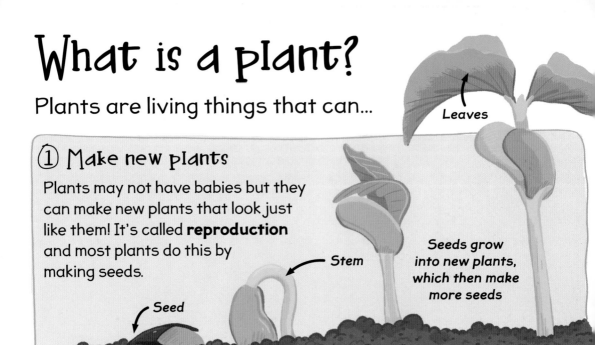

Leaves

① Make new plants

Plants may not have babies but they can make new plants that look just like them! It's called **reproduction** and most plants do this by making seeds.

Stem

Seed

Seeds grow into new plants, which then make more seeds

② Breathe

Plants **breathe** air through tiny holes in their leaves.

We breathe in carbon dioxide from the air and breathe out oxygen.

③ Get rid of waste

Plants are brilliant because when they breathe they make a **waste** gas called oxygen — it's the gas we need to stay alive!

Thanks for giving me clean air to breathe!

④ Use senses

A plant may not have eyes but it can sense light and it can feel, smell, hear and...

⑤ ...move

Plants **move** their leaves to face the Sun. Seeds **travel** too. Some of them are carried a long way on the wind.

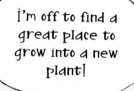

I'm off to find a great place to grow into a new plant!

⑥ Get food

Some plants eat bugs, but most of them make their own **food**. They use this to...

I'm a sticky sundew plant catching insects for my dinner!

From little acorns...

...mighty oaks can grow.

⑦ ...grow

Most plants — even giant trees — start their lives as seeds, but they soon grow and change.

Do plants get hungry?

Plants don't feel hungry the same way that animals do, but they do need food. Animals eat their food, but plants make all the food they need.

Flowering plant

Sunlight

i can store the food i make in different parts of me and save it for the winter.

Flower

Leaf

Stem

Oxygen out

Carbon dioxide in

Why are leaves green?

Because they have a green substance called chlorophyll inside them. This helps the plant collect the energy from sunlight and turn it into food.

Plants use sunlight to turn water and carbon dioxide from the air into food. This is called photosynthesis.

Water is sucked up from the soil by a plant's roots

Roots also suck up minerals to help a plant grow

How do plants feed the world?

Plants are the beginning of most food chains. This is when living things depend on each other for food. Animals eat plants – fruits, vegetables, nuts and seeds – and some animals also eat other animals.

A food chain shows how energy and nutrients pass from one living thing to another.

I turn the Sun's energy into my food.

I get my energy from eating plants.

Eating small animals and plants gives me the energy to run and play.

Winter

Spring

Autumn

Summer

Why do plants lose their leaves?

In the autumn many leaves change colour and fall off. This is so the plant can store up water and energy over the winter, ready to grow new leaves in the spring.

Did you know?

Plants are cool! When they absorb **sunlight** to make their food they make the air cooler. This helps to control the Earth's temperature.

Solar panels work just like **leaves** because they collect energy from sunlight. We use that energy to make electricity.

Nutrients are the foods, minerals and vitamins we need to live and grow.

Mimosa plants are shy! If something touches them they quickly fold up their leaves. It's a clever way to avoid being eaten.

Eating **bananas** can make you happy! They contain nutrients that help you to feel good and sleep well.

Yuk!

Argh!

When some plants hear the sound of **caterpillars** munching nearby they make nasty tasting chemicals so the caterpillars leave them alone!

The largest leaves belong to **arum plants**. Some have heart-shaped leaves that grow more than 3 metres wide.

Just one **elephant** eats 200 kilograms of plant food every day.

I'm a Japanese morning glory and I change from purple to blue throughout the day.

Some flowers get a suntan! They **change colour** through the day as they warm up.

Mmm, you smell nice. I'm going to wrap myself around you.

Plants don't have noses but some of them can smell. **Dodder plants** grow on other plants. They sniff out their favourites and grow towards them!

Which plants snap, munch and stick?

Yum!

Some plants don't just make food from sunlight. They eat things too! They are called carnivorous, or meat-eating, plants.

We live in dark, boggy places where there's not much sunlight to help make our food, so we eat small creatures to survive.

How do plants catch bugs?

Venus flytraps have trap-shaped leaves coated in hairs. When a spider, beetle or fly crawls over the hairs, the plant's trap snaps shut! The bug tries to escape, but there is no way out.

Snap!

Venus flytrap

Which plants drown their food?

Pitcher plants grow jug-shaped leaves that fill with water. Small creatures are tempted by the plant's smell and fall in, often drowning in the liquid at the bottom of the 'jug'.

Some pitcher plants are big enough to catch frogs and mice!

Stick!

Pitcher Plant

Which plants trap with glue?

Sundew Plant

Once i trap my prey, i make liquid that dissolves the bug into a gloopy soup.

Sundew plants have delicious-looking red droplets that attract passing bugs. They are actually sticky glue, and when a bug lands on them it sticks. The plant then folds over and begins to dissolve the bug. Yum!

Why are flowers pretty?

Flowers have a very important job to do – it's called pollination – and many of them need insects to help. Colours, smells and shapes of flowers attract insects to a plant to pollinate it.

Pollen grows on stamens – the male parts of a flower

Pollen lands here and grows a tube down to the ovary to make new seeds

Colourful petals attract insects

Pollen grains are tiny and look like yellow or orange dust

What is pollination?

Plants make pollen. It comes from the male part of a flower and joins with a flower's egg to make a new plant seed. Insects carry pollen from one flower to another flower's eggs. This is called pollination.

Eggs are inside a flower's ovary. This is the female part of a flower

Flowers make nectar at the bottom of petals. It's a sugary liquid that bugs love!

Why do bees have baskets?

Some bees have special
pouches on their legs that
they use as baskets
to carry the
pollen they collect
from flowers.

i gather pollen
from flowers to
use as food in my
bee colony.

Bee

Pollen

Banana
flower

Bat

Why do bananas
need bats?

Banana, cocoa and mango
plants are pollinated by bats.
They visit the flowers to
drink nectar, get covered in
pollen and carry it from plant
to plant. Birds and moths also
pollinate some plants.

i smell sweet
at night to tempt
moths to come and
pollinate me.

Moth

Honeysuckle

How many?

1

The number of days it takes a swarm of locusts to munch through 190,000 tonnes of plants.

The world's tallest flowering plant is a eucalyptus tree called Centurion that grows in Australia. It's **100** metres tall!

2000

The age in years of an ancient seed found by scientists. They planted it and it grew into a healthy magnolia tree!

It takes just **1/50th** of a second for the bladderwort pond plant to catch mosquito larvae in its traps.

I am the fastest killer in the plant kingdom!

150 years old – the age of a giant bromeliad before it grows its first flower. It dies afterwards.

It can take **10** days for a Venus flytrap to digest a dead bug.

A saguaro cactus grows just **4** centimetres in ten years, but bamboo can grow **90** centimetres in a single day!

200

The number of litres of water one corn plant needs to grow. That's more than two full bathtubs!

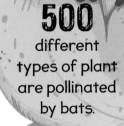

500 different types of plant are pollinated by bats.

There are **12,500** different types of tree growing in the Amazon rainforest.

Why are tomatoes red?

Tomatoes and other fruits are colourful to tell animals that they are ripe and ready to eat.

I'm tiny and green because I'm not ready to eat!

Tomato plant

Fruits have seeds in them. When animals eat the fruits, and then do a poo, they spread the seeds to new places where they grow into new plants.

I'm red, plump, juicy and sweet. Eat me!

Apple

Seeds

Warning!

Only eat fruits and nuts you have been told are safe to eat.

Why do fruits grow?

When a plant grows some new seeds, the fruit of the plant grows around the seeds to protect them.

Can seeds grow inside me?

Seeds can't grow inside animals or people. They need soil, water and oxygen to start growing.

Water goes into the seed and it swells

There is food in the seed for the new plant

Why are nuts hard?

Nuts are hard fruits. They are hard to protect the seeds inside, or to help them move safely to new places.

Squirrel

Agouti

I'm the only animal with teeth strong enough to break open a Brazil nut pod to reach the nuts inside.

I bury acorns so I can eat them in winter. If I forget where I put them they can grow into oak trees!

Have you ever tried to grow a seed? It's easy peasy!

The seedling has a shoot and little leaves

Pea plant

The new plant starts to grow

Roots grow into the soil to collect more water and stop the plant from blowing away

241

Did Diplodocus eat flowers?

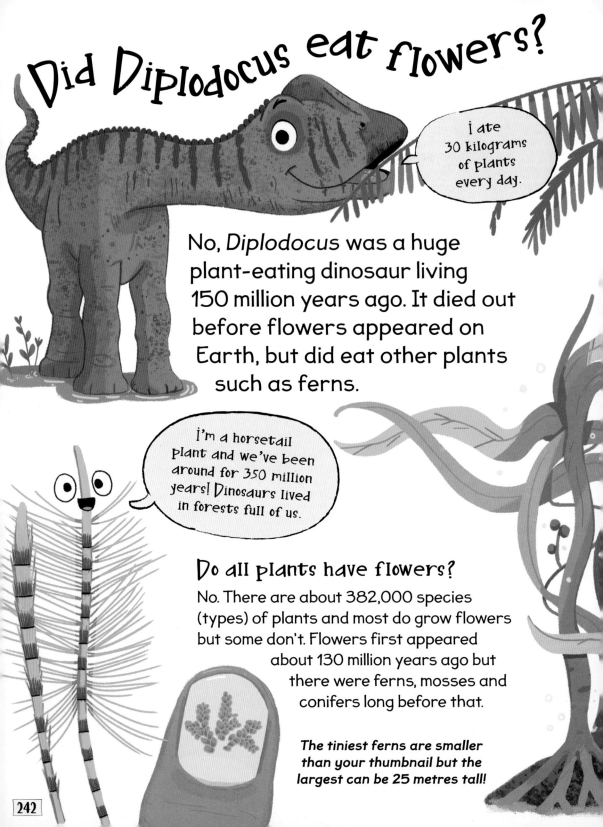

I ate 30 kilograms of plants every day.

No, *Diplodocus* was a huge plant-eating dinosaur living 150 million years ago. It died out before flowers appeared on Earth, but did eat other plants such as ferns.

I'm a horsetail plant and we've been around for 350 million years! Dinosaurs lived in forests full of us.

Do all plants have flowers?

No. There are about 382,000 species (types) of plants and most do grow flowers but some don't. Flowers first appeared about 130 million years ago but there were ferns, mosses and conifers long before that.

The tiniest ferns are smaller than your thumbnail but the largest can be 25 metres tall!

What is an evergreen?

It's a plant that keeps its leaves all year round. Conifers are evergreen trees that are often triangular — the perfect shape for growing in snowy places, as snow slips right off the branches without snapping them!

Conifers grow their seeds inside cones instead of in flowers or fruits

Pine trees, redwoods and fir trees are all types of conifer.

Kelp use sticky pads to fix themselves to the rocks or the seabed.

Can plants grow in the sea?

Yes! Seaweeds belong to a group of plants called algae. Giant kelp is the world's biggest seaweed and it grows in undersea forests. A single strand of kelp can grow to 30 metres long!

How do plants stay safe?

Many animals eat plants, and that's not good news for our green friends! They need to defend themselves from attack and some use prickly thorns and poisons to do this.

Spiky thorns!

Who hugs trees to death?

i do! i'm a strangler fig. i wrap myself around a tall tree to hold me up. Eventually, the tree dies, but i survive!

Deadly nightshade

Warning!

Only eat berries you have been told are safe to eat.

Why are some berries deadly?

Berries often look tasty, but some contain poison to put animals off eating them. Deadly nightshade and foxglove plants can stop your heart from beating, but doctors can also make medicines from them.

Strangler fig

Cactus

My fat stem stores water as it rarely rains in a desert. I'm covered in needle-like leaves called spines.

I'm a prickly sweet chestnut. My case only cracks open when the nuts inside are ripe to be eaten by animals who then spread my seeds far and wide.

What's the point of thorns and prickles?

Many plants have sharp thorns and prickles to stop animals from eating them.

Sweet chestnut

We are soft, juicy and tasty, so many animals would like to eat us – but we have a surprise for them!

Nettle

Ouch!

Why do nettles sting?

Nettles have tiny stinging hairs, each with a bead of acid on its tip. If you touch a nettle the hairs prick your skin and the beads release the acid.

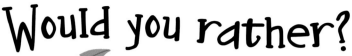

Would you rather?

Would you rather sit under a **palm tree** where coconuts might fall on your head, or swim through the roots of a **mangrove tree** where young crocodiles live?

Would you rather be able to make **plants** grow quickly or make it **rain** whenever you want?

It's time to sleep. Would you prefer to lie down in a leaf tent with a **Honduran white bat**...

...or in a grass house with a **harvest mouse**?

Would you rather munch on **bugs** like a Venus flytrap...

Would you rather live to be hundreds of years old like a **cypress tree**...

...or grow to be 9 metres tall like the tallest **sunflower**?

...or be a pitcher plant that eats **frogs**?

Would you rather drink coffee made with **civet poo** or eat durian fruit that smells of **old socks**?

Why do giraffes have long tongues?

Giraffes have long, thick tongues that they wrap around a prickly acacia tree to eat its leaves. Acacia trees don't like having their leaves eaten by giraffes, so they also make yummy food for biting ants.

Ouch!

Durian fruits smell like a mixture of dead fish, smelly socks and poo, but I don't mind. I know the flesh inside is delicious!

If a giraffe tries to eat the acacia leaves we can bite its nose!

Acacia leaves contain sweet nectar that ants love to eat

Yum!

Acacia tree

Why is the durian fruit so smelly?

The big, prickly durian fruit stinks so that animals who like it can easily sniff it out and eat it. They then spread its seeds over a wide area in their poo.

Yum!

Sea slug

Sea grapes seaweed

Why do slugs dress up as plants?

This sea slug looks just like its favourite food — sea grapes seaweed! The slug uses this food to turn itself green and even grows lumps on its back for camouflage as it feeds!

Which plants stink of rotting socks?

Lots of plants make foul smells — and some smell like rotting socks! What's more, some animals love this! Arums often smell like rotting meat to attract flies, which buzz among the arums pollinating them.

My flowers grow 3 metres tall to spread my foul smell far and wide.

Yuk!

Titan arum

How big is the tallest tree?

The tallest tree is a coast redwood called Hyperion in California, USA, and it's taller than a 27-storey building! It is about 116 metres tall, and it grows 4 centimetres taller every year. How much have you grown in the past year?

I have more than 550 million leaves!

Coast redwood

Why do people hug trees?

You can hug a tree to work out how big and how old it is. As trees age they get taller but their trunks also get wider. If it takes six children or more to hug an oak tree then it's very old.

Is a mushroom a plant?

No, mushrooms are a type of fungus but, like plants and animals, they are alive. They can grow on dead trees using the wood as their food.

Mushrooms

Warning!
Some mushrooms are very poisonous to eat.

Deathwatch beetle

When we hatch from eggs we eat the tasty wood.

Larvae

I'm tapping on this dead tree so a female can find me! She'll lay her eggs in the rotting wood.

What's that knocking sound?

It's a deathwatch beetle inside rotting wood tapping to attract a mate! In the forest, dead trees and logs make a great place for insects to live and start a family.

Who loves plants?

We do! We eat plants. We also use them for lots of other things...

We use **wood** to make paper and cardboard. Books are made from **trees**!

Oil is made from lots of different plants — such as sunflowers, olives and soybeans — and used for **cooking**.

Rubber is collected from rubber trees. It's turned into lots of things, such as **toys**, tyres and boots.

We use the **wood** from trees to make **furniture**.

Wood is burned to make fires for **cooking** food and for **heating** homes.

Dead plants can be put onto a **compost** heap. When they rot they put nutrients back into the soil, so more plants can grow.

Plants help to **clean our air** by absorbing carbon dioxide, and they help to keep our planet cool, too. This means they can help us to reduce climate change.

Cotton plants grow fluffy cases around their seeds. These are turned into cotton fabric, which is made into **clothes**.

Scientists use plants to make new **medicines** to help treat diseases.

A compendium of questions

How do piranha fish help rainforests grow?

Some piranhas eat fallen fruit from rainforest trees. They poo out the seeds in the river, which then grow into new trees.

Do plants scream?

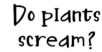

No, but long ago people believed that a mandrake plant screamed when it was pulled from the ground, and that anyone who heard it would drop dead!

Why do people count tree rings?

A tree grows a new ring every year, so you can count the number of rings on a tree stump to see how old it is.

Can a plant live in space?

Yes. On the International Space Station scientists have grown lettuces, peas and courgettes.

Why do caterpillars eat poisonous leaves?

Monarch caterpillars eat poisonous milkweed plants and store the poisons in their bodies, so birds won't eat them.

Yum!

How deep do roots grow?

Plants that grow in very dry places need long roots to reach any water they can find deep in the soil. One fig tree had roots that spread 122 metres down!

What is an upside down tree?

Baobabs are sometimes called upside-down trees because their short, thick branches look like roots. They grow smelly flowers to tempt bats to come and pollinate them.

What is the largest flower?

The rafflesia plant grows the biggest single flower in the world. It can be more than a metre wide and smells like rotting meat.

What's the largest seed in the world?

The seeds of a coco-de-mer tree can be 50 centimetres wide and weigh up to 30 kilograms!

Ew!

What is a pterosaur?

Answer on page 275

Which dinosaur LiKED stinky smells?

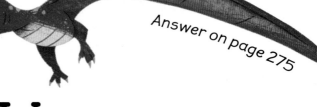

Answer on page 285

Who collects dino POO?

Answer on page 282

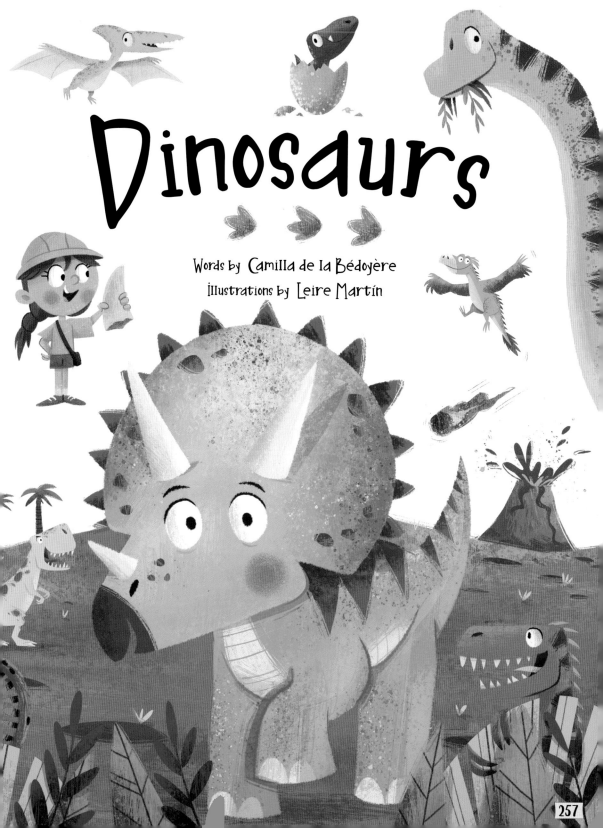

Dinosaurs

Words by Camilla de la Bédoyère

Illustrations by Leire Martín

When did dinosaurs live?

The first dinosaurs lived about 240 million years ago, long before there were people. Dinosaurs evolved from other animals called dinosauromorphs. They were cat-sized reptiles.

i'm a dinosauromorph. When an animal evolves it changes over time, so it can survive in a changing world.

i'm one of the first dinosaurs. i lived about 230 million years ago.

Herrerasaurus

Tarbosaurus

i'm one of the last dinosaurs. i roamed the planet 70 million years ago.

Were all dinosaurs huge?

Dinosaurs came in all shapes and sizes. The largest ones were called titanosaurs. They were more than 20 metres long and weighed as much as six elephants!

I'm one of the biggest dinosaurs ever. Can you guess where in the world I came from?

Argentinosaurus

This tiny terror is Microraptor. It is just 40–60 centimetres long

Being small helps me to glide from trees.

Where did they live?

The first dinosaurs lived on Pangaea — a single, giant slab of land. The world was very hot and dry and there was just one ocean called Panthalassa. Dinosaurs could walk all the way from the North Pole to the South Pole. We call this time in Earth's history the Triassic.

PANGAEA

Who would be at a dino party?

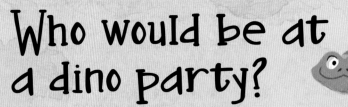

Dinosaurs were reptiles, so they might invite other reptiles. These baby *Maiasaura* have just hatched, so they are sharing their birthday party. Can you spot which guests are not dinosaurs?

Maiasaura

Who looked after the babies?

Maiasaura mums took good care of their nests, eggs and young. They protected them from hungry *Troodon.*

Watch out kids, that hungry Troodon has its big eyes on you!

Troodon was an intelligent dinosaur with big eyes and sharp claws

Why do dinos have such strange names?

Dinosaur names are often made up of more than one word. Put together, the words tell us more about the dinosaur.

Carcharodontosaurus
shark-tooth-lizard

Tyrannosaurus rex
tyrant-lizard-king

Guanlong crown-dragon

Maiasaura good mother-lizard

Triceratops three-horned-face

Torosaurus bull-lizard

Mei long sleeping-dragon

Hey, who is Tyrannosaurus rex?

Mei long was covered in bird-like feathers and may have been very colourful

Did dinosaurs have fur?

No, dinosaurs didn't have fur but many of them had feathers. The feathers were often fluffy, but some dinosaurs grew long feathers, like modern birds. Fuzzy, fluffy feathers kept dinosaurs warm.

Yutyrannus was up to 9 metres long and covered in fuzzy feathers

Did you know?

A fully-grown *T rex* was **longer** and **heavier** than a bus and its skull was so heavy you'd need a forklift truck to pick it up.

In 1824 **Megalosaurus** was the first dinosaur to be named. When its thighbone was dug up people thought it belonged to a human giant!

Meat-eating dinosaurs had long, curved, sharp teeth.

Titanosaurs were huge, long-necked dinosaurs but they were not the largest animals to ever live. The **blue whale**, which lives in our oceans today, wins that prize.

Plant-eaters had peg-like or spoon-shaped teeth.

All dinos could **walk**, some of them could **swim** and others — like *Microraptor* — could **glide** between trees.

Dinosaurs didn't have **kneecaps**, but no one knows why!

T rex and *Tarbosaurus* might have made good **ballet dancers** — they balanced beautifully on their tiptoes!

Ichthyosaurs were fast-swimming reptiles that lived in the sea. They looked like whales or dolphins, but were related to **snakes** and **lizards**.

Which dinosaurs had the longest necks?

Sauropods were a group of huge dinosaurs with very long necks, like *Brachiosaurus*. Having a long neck meant that sauropods could reach high up into trees to eat leaves. They might spend all day eating.

Mamenchisaurus had a long, thin neck that was 12 metres in length

Mamenchisaurus

Brachiosaurus

Parasaurolophus

Could dinosaurs roaaarr?

No one knows what sounds dinosaurs made. They may have roared, growled, chirped, tweeted — or made no sounds at all. *Parasaurolophus* had a long, hollow crest on its head. It may have blown air through the crest to make honking sounds — like a trumpet!

Diplodocus

Diplodocus *had a long, bendy tail too, which it used to wallop other dinosaurs*

Do you think I'm handsome?

Oviraptor

Some dinosaurs liked to look good! Horns, frills, head plates and colourful feathers or skin may have all helped male dinosaurs look attractive to female ones.

Who was king of the dinosaurs?

Look out! Here comes *Tyrannosaurus rex* — king of the dinosaurs. *T rex* was a massive 13 metres long and weighed about 7 tonnes — that makes it one of the biggest meat-eaters that's ever lived on land, in the whole history of the planet!

T rex may have hunted in groups. A pack of them would have been a terrifying sight for a Triceratops like me!

Yikes!

How scary was a T rex?

T rex was one of the scariest dinosaurs to ever live. It was a huge, fearsome, powerful hunter that preyed on other big dinosaurs. It could bite its prey so hard it snapped bones.

Sharp claws on hands and feet

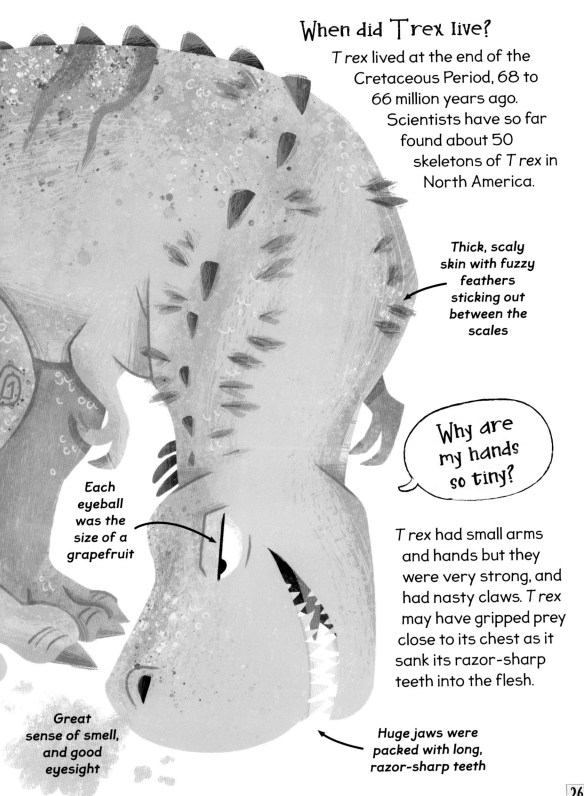

When did T rex live?

T rex lived at the end of the Cretaceous Period, 68 to 66 million years ago. Scientists have so far found about 50 skeletons of T rex in North America.

Thick, scaly skin with fuzzy feathers sticking out between the scales

Why are my hands so tiny?

T rex had small arms and hands but they were very strong, and had nasty claws. T rex may have gripped prey close to its chest as it sank its razor-sharp teeth into the flesh.

Each eyeball was the size of a grapefruit

Great sense of smell, and good eyesight

Huge jaws were packed with long, razor-sharp teeth

How many?

3

The number of claws *Therizinosaurus* had on each hand — the longest was 71 centimetres long! It probably used its claws to grab branches and pull leaves to its mouth.

10

The size in centimetres of the smallest known dinosaur eggs. The biggest were 30 centimetres long — twice as big as an ostrich egg.

50

The number of new species of dinosaur being discovered every year.

In 1905 the bones of a *T rex* were put on display in a museum for the first time. Scientists thought they were just **8 million** years old!

T rex could run at speeds of about **30** kilometres an hour — that's faster than an elephant but much slower than a racehorse.

Most dinos probably grew quickly and died before they reached the age of

30.

The world was about **6°** Celsius hotter during the Cretaceous than it is today. The hot, steamy weather meant that lush forests could grow as far as the North Pole!

19 The number of bones in the neck of Mamenchisaurus – more than any dinosaur discovered so far.

2 The weight in kilograms that a 10-year-old *T rex* would have gained every day! A newly hatched *T rex* would have been the size of pigeon, but it grew super fast.

The Jurassic Period lasted **55 million** years. Then Pangaea began to break up into big chunks of land called continents.

How did dinosaurs defend themselves?

Many plant-eating dinosaurs had bony armour to protect them from attack. Thick slabs of bone, plates, scales, spikes and bony bumps all helped ankylosaurs fend off the razor-sharp claws and dagger-like teeth of meat-eating dinosaurs.

Ankylosaurus

Why is there a big club on your tail?

Smash!

I'm an ankylosaur from the Late Cretaceous. I have a huge club on the end of my tail and it's very useful for walloping anything that attacks me — like that Trex over there!

What did dinosaurs eat?

Some dinosaurs hunted animals to eat, other dinosaurs ate plants, and some ate whatever they could find!

I'm fully armed with slashing, gripping claws and jaws lined with razor-sharp teeth. I'm fast, smart... and hungry for meat!

Sauropelta

Raptors, like Deinonychus, were light on their feet and super speedy

I eat plants. My body is covered in bony plates and spikes that make it difficult for Deinonychus to attack me!

How much did T rex eat?

Yum!

T rex was a hungry beast that needed about 110 kilograms of meat a day. That's more than 1000 burgers!

Plant-eaters like me graze on low-growing plants and leaves. Even our teeth are shaped like leaves!

I look like an ostrich with my long legs, feathers and toothless beak. I mostly peck at bugs, lizards and other small animals.

Deinonychus

Ornithomimus

How fast could a dinosaur run?

Plant-eating dinosaurs were slow movers, but most predator dinosaurs needed speed to hunt and catch their prey.

Ornithomimus was one of the fastest dinosaurs, with top speeds of 35 kilometres an hour or more

273

Could dinosaurs fly?

Yes, and they still do! Flying dinosaurs are all around us. We call them birds.

Over a long time, some dinosaurs began to develop bird-like bodies with wings and feathers. By 150 million years ago, the first birds had appeared. That means all birds are actually dinosaurs!

What was the first bird called?

Archaeopteryx – that's me! I have teeth, claws on my wings and a long, bony tail. I can climb, run, glide and even fly a little.

I lived 130 million years ago. I could glide between trees and flap my wings.

Microraptor

Quetzalcoatlus

I'm a giant pterosaur. I have a wingspan of 12 metres and I'm one of the biggest animals to ever fly – one of my feet is bigger than a human's leg!

What is a pterosaur?

Pterosaurs were flying reptiles that lived at the same time as the dinosaurs. Their wings were made of thin skin, spread out between the bones in their arms and fingers, and they were superb flyers.

Would you rather?

Have a **Maiasaura** or **Majungatholus** for a mum? Scientists think that *Majungatholus* may have eaten members of its own family!

Fight a *T rex* or **fly** with a pterosaur?

Be a **fast-running** Gallimimus or a **slow-moving** Stegosaurus?

Have **teeth** like *T rex* or a **neck** like *Supersaurus*? You'd either need a very big toothbrush, or a very long scarf!

If you had the body of a sauropod would you use your long tail to **splash** in water, or let people **slide** down it?

Be as **big** as Brachiosaurus or as **small** as Microraptor?

Be covered in a coat of **soft, fluffy feathers** or have **scary horns** growing on your face?

Have tea with a *Tarbosaurus*, **cuddle** a *Carcharodontosaurus* or **stroke** a *Stegosaurus*?

277

How could sauropods grow so big?

Sauropods were giant plant-eaters. They had big bones and huge muscles to move their bodies. They also had holes and air sacs in their bones, which kept them light. Without these, sauropods would have been even heavier!

Could a dinosaur crush a car?

Argentinosaurus weighed over 60 tonnes. If it sat on a car, it could crush it in an instant! *T rex* had one of the most powerful bites of any animal ever known. It could have crushed a car in its mighty jaws!

Crunch!

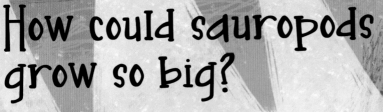

Brachiosaurus

I am three times taller than a giraffe!

How did dinosaurs kill their prey?

They were equipped with some lethal weapons! Claws, jaws, teeth and tails could all be used to injure, catch or kill other animals. Raptors had long, curved claws on their feet for slashing and slicing.

What happened to the dinosaurs?

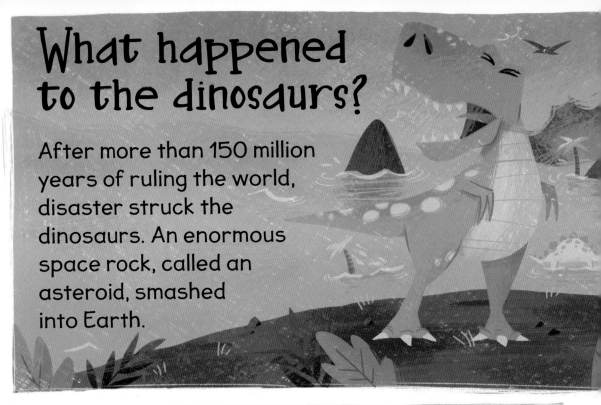

After more than 150 million years of ruling the world, disaster struck the dinosaurs. An enormous space rock, called an asteroid, smashed into Earth.

How did Earth change?

It turned cold and dark, and there was very little food because plants couldn't grow. Over the next few thousand years, most types of animals, including the dinosaurs, went extinct.

The dinosaurs began to die, along with many other animals

The asteroid hit Earth with the explosive force of a billion giant bombs

There were giant waves, floods and burning winds before dark clouds of dust filled the sky

Are the dinosaurs still alive?

Yes they are! Birds belong to the dinosaur family, and some survived the asteroid, along with other animals. Today, more than 10,000 different types of bird live all over the world.

Eagles have sharp claws and beaks like many dinosaurs did

Huge, flightless terror birds lived in South America about two million years ago

Can you believe I'm a dinosaur? RAAA!

Ducks, geese and chickens are dinosaur relatives

Who collects dino poo?

① This dinosaur died and its soft parts rotted away

We do! We're palaeontologists (say: pal-ee-on-tol-oh-jists). We look for the remains of animals that lived long ago.

What's a fossil?

A fossil is the remains of an animal that has turned to stone over millions of years.

② Its bones were covered in sand or mud

We look at fossils of bones and footprints. Fossil poo helps us to work out what dinosaurs ate.

Where can I find dinosaurs?

Lots of museums have dinosaur fossils you can look at. They are being dug up all over the world, from the USA to China! Mudstone, sandstone and limestone are all good rocks in which to find fossils.

Whose tooth is that?

It's a fossilized tooth from a Trex! Each adult had 50 massive teeth and they could grow new ones if the old ones fell out or broke.

③
Over time, the bones were buried by more sand or mud and turned to stone — they have been fossilized

My bones are revealed when land erodes (wears away).

283

A compendium of questions

What was the biggest scary dinosaur to ever live?

It may have been the super scary *Spinosaurus*. It was probably longer and heavier than *T rex*, and its huge head had crocodile-like jaws lined with teeth.

How many types of dinosaur are there?

About 2000 types have been found and named so far, but there are plenty more to discover.

Why did Brachiosaurus eat stones?

Like many reptiles, *Brachiosaurus* probably swallowed stones to help grind up tough plant food in its stomach.

Were dinosaurs clever?

Some were! *Troodon* had a big brain for its size. It was smarter than a turtle but not as clever as a parrot.

Could I out-run a Velociraptor?

No! *Velociraptor* could reach speeds of 35 kilometres an hour. Few animals could escape those razor-sharp claws!

Were pterosaurs flying dinosaurs?

Pterosaurs could fly but they were not dinosaurs. They belonged to a group of reptiles that appeared before the first dinosaurs.

Which dino could fish?

Deinocheirus could. It had very long arms and sharp claws. It may have reached into rivers to grab fish or reached high into trees to pick fruit.

Which dinosaur loved stinky smells?

Tarbosaurus was a hunter, but also ate dead animals that it found by following the stench of rotting flesh.

Were any dinosaurs friendly?

Some dinosaurs, like *Iguanodon*, probably lived peacefully in herds. *T rex* might have hunted in packs, but was probably not friendly!

Why do whales SPOUT water?

Answer on page 312

How SMART is an octopus?

Answer on page 314

Which fish ties itself in KNOTS?

Answer on page 314

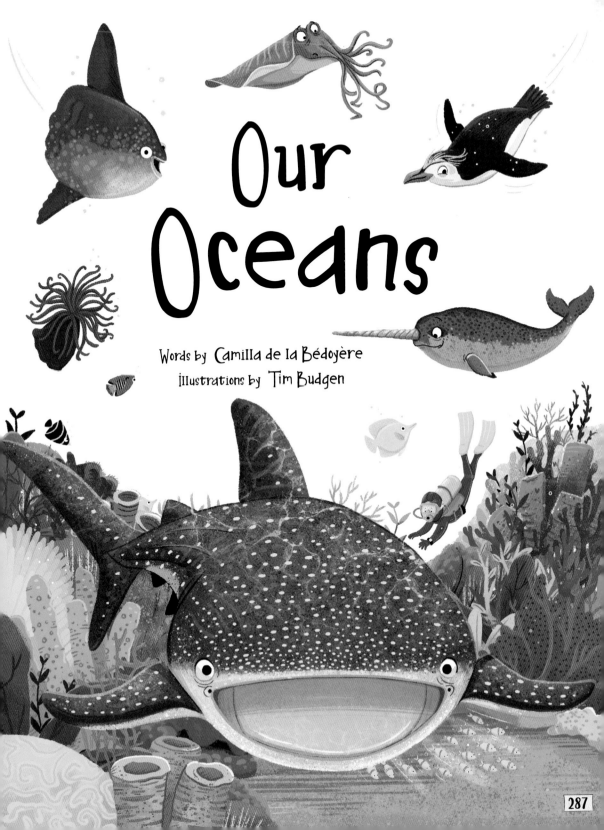

Our Oceans

Words by Camilla de la Bédoyère

Illustrations by Tim Budgen

How big is an ocean?

There are five oceans and they are all HUGE! Together, they cover two thirds of Earth's surface.

NORTH AMERICA

ATLANTIC OCEAN

An ocean is a large area of salty water. It's also called the sea.

PACIFIC OCEAN

SOUTH AMERICA

Seaweeds are plants that live in salty water.

Day octopus

SOUTHERN OCEAN

Long-snouted seahorse

Are the oceans important?

Yes, billions of animals and plants live in them! People use the things that live in the ocean for all sorts of things, too. A type of seaweed called red algae is used in peanut butter — it makes it easy to spread!

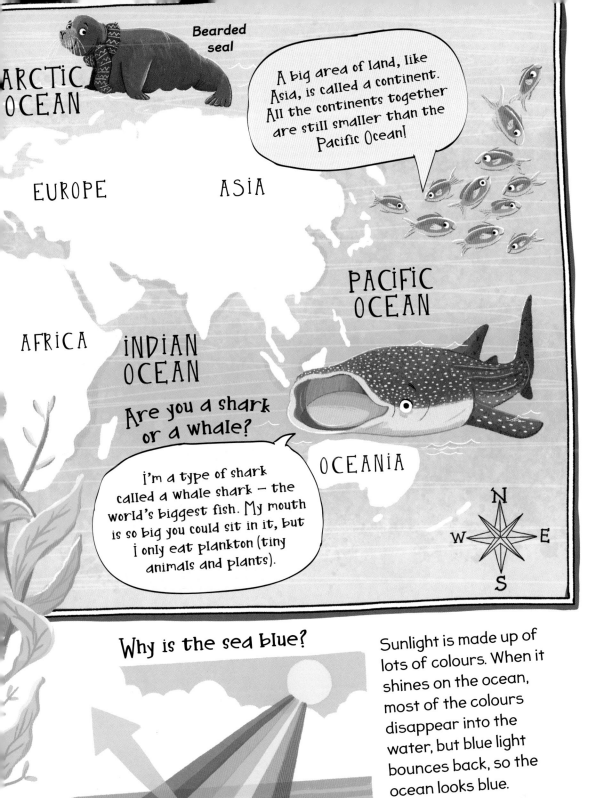

ARCTIC OCEAN

Bearded seal

A big area of land, like Asia, is called a continent. All the continents together are still smaller than the Pacific Ocean!

EUROPE

ASIA

PACIFIC OCEAN

AFRICA

INDIAN OCEAN

Are you a shark or a whale?

I'm a type of shark called a whale shark — the world's biggest fish. My mouth is so big you could sit in it, but I only eat plankton (tiny animals and plants).

OCEANIA

N
W   E
S

Why is the sea blue?

Sunlight is made up of lots of colours. When it shines on the ocean, most of the colours disappear into the water, but blue light bounces back, so the ocean looks blue.

What is a fish?

Fish are animals that have skeletons, gills and fins. There are more than 32,000 types, and most of them live in oceans.

Tail fin swishes from side to side when swimming

Overlapping scales are smooth and slippery

Herring

I'm the perfect shape for swimming. My silvery scales help water to flow easily over my skin.

Slim, sleek body moves quickly through water

Can people breathe underwater too?

No – sorry! You need to breathe air because you have lungs. All fish have special organs called gills that work in water.

Water and air have oxygen gas in them. All animals need oxygen to live.

Oxygen-rich water flows in

Triggerfish

Water flows out over the gills, where the oxygen passes into the fish's blood

Do fish have special homes?

Some do. Clownfish live among the tentacles of stinging sea anemones. The fish are covered in special slime that protects them from stings, but animals that might want to eat them can't get close!

I can glide for up to 200 metres.

Can fish fly?

No – but some can glide. Flying fish have very streamlined bodies and use their big fins to launch out of the water into the air.

Whoosh!

How is my nose like a shark?

Most fish skeletons are made of bone. Shark skeletons are made of cartilage, which is softer than bone. Our noses and ears have cartilage – that's why they're bendy!

Bull shark

Did you know?

At 3 metres long, the ocean **sunfish** is one of the world's biggest bony fish.

A **hairy frogfish** is a fast eater. It sucks food into its mouth like a vacuum cleaner — 50 times faster than the blink of an eye!

Octopuses can turn red when they are angry.

Electric rays can zap fish with an electric shock. Once the fish has been stunned, the ray can eat it!

Seaweed is often used as a thickener in ice cream!

The **sperm whale** has the biggest brain on the planet — and probably the whole Universe!

500 million years ago the only living things on Earth were in the ocean.

Baby sharks and baby seals are called **pups**, and baby fish are called **fry**.

Shark skin feels like sandpaper. It is covered in tiny bumpy scales that help them slip through the water.

I'm more like a hippo than a herring!

Whales and **dolphins** aren't fish – they are mammals.

North Pole

A **great white shark** can eat enough meat to make 3000 burgers in one go, and it won't want to eat again for at least ten days.

Polar bears and **penguins** never meet because penguins live near the South Pole and polar bears live near the North Pole!

It's like looking in a mirror!

South Pole

Sailors used to think that **dugongs** were mermaids. They're actually plump mammals that spend their time grazing on sea plants.

Do trees grow in the deep sea?

No — but giant kelp seaweed grows in huge forests! It is found in the Pacific Ocean, and can grow up to 50 centimetres in one day.

Bumps contain air that helps the kelp to float

A kelp forest is a great place to hide — one strand can be more than 30 metres long.

We are lizards that live on the Galapagos Islands in the Pacific Ocean.

Who picnics at the bottom of the sea?

Marine iguanas do! They dive to depths of 12 metres — and stay there for up to an hour while they nibble on seaweed that grows on the seabed.

Do baby fish go to nursery?

Young fish and reptiles keep away from predators in special hiding places called nurseries. Shallow waters around sea grasses and mangrove tree roots make good nurseries.

Sea otters can wrap themselves in kelp so they don't float away

Mangrove trees grow at the coast, with their roots in shallow salty water.

Sea creatures sometimes mistake plastic floating in the ocean for food. If we eat it, it can kill us.

What do turtles eat?

Green sea turtles feast on fields of sea grasses that grow underwater.

Baby turtles hide from sharks in the sea grasses

Who plays hide and seek?

Many ocean animals do! On coral reefs, millions of sea creatures live close together. Lots of them use clever tricks to avoid being eaten by the others.

I look like seaweed. I'm a type of fish called a leafy seadragon.

I'm a sea slug — aren't I beautiful? My lovely colours tell animals that I am poisonous.

I'm a decorator crab, and I'm holding onto a piece of coral as a clever disguise.

I'm a cuttlefish and I can change colour in a flash.

Do fish need friends?

My best friend is a busy little shrimp. I'm a coral grouper and my friend cleans my teeth.

I also nibble away any dead skin. Yum!

We moray eels have long, thin bodies and can hide in cracks in the coral. We eat almost anything we can catch.

Can you see a reef from space?
Yes! The Great Barrier Reef stretches over 2000 kilometres off the coast of Australia. Reefs are built by tiny animals called polyps. Each one lives in its own rocky cup, waving its tentacles in the water.

It took thousands of years for polyps like me to build the Great Barrier Reef.

297

How long does it take to make an island?

If a volcano erupts on the seabed, it can make an island in a few years! Lava (a type of liquid rock) pours out and builds up to create a brand new island.

Volcano erupts on seabed

A cone shape of lava forms on the seabed

The cone grows so big it breaks the surface — it's a new island!

Can I find treasure on an island?

Yes — but not the sort that belongs to pirates! The treasure to be found on islands is all the precious animals that live on them.

We're baby hawksbill turtles. Our mum laid eggs in a nest and then swam away. Now we're hatching.

We're leaving our nest and heading to the sea.

I fly to islands when it's time to build my nest and lay eggs. I'm an albatross, and I'm huge.

Black and white ruffed lemur

Who lives on an island?

Islands are often home to animals that live nowhere else on Earth. About 60 types of lemur live only on the island of Madagascar, which is in the Indian Ocean.

Christmas island, near Australia, swarms with millions of red crabs. We lay our eggs in the sea.

Giant tortoises like me are found on coral islands in the Indian Ocean. We can live to be more than 100 years old!

How many?

I'm one of the longest animals ever!

About **100 million** sharks are killed by people every year.

10 metres The length of a bootlace worm.

400 million

The number of years that sharks have lived in the oceans.

There are more volcanoes under the sea than on land! **452** are on the edges of the Pacific Ocean.

Pufferfish have poisonous flesh. About **30** people die every year after eating them.

7 metres

The length of the biggest saltwater crocodiles.

A single one of my teeth can be more than 10 centimetres in length!

A starfish can have more than **30** arms!

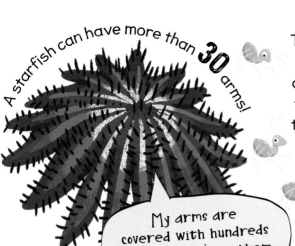

> My arms are covered with hundreds of tiny feet. I use them to walk on the seabed.

There were **40 million** crabs on Christmas Island — until yellow crazy ants arrived. They spray the crabs with acid and eat them, so far killing about **15 million** of them.

507

...the incredible age in years of a clam that was found in the Atlantic Ocean.

Phew!

40,000

...the number of eggs a herring can lay in one go.

A narwhal's giant tooth can reach **3 metres** in length.

350
The number of types of coral that live in the Great Barrier Reef.

> That's why it's important to cut down the amount of plastic you use, and to recycle it.

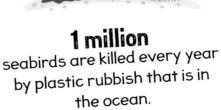

1 million
seabirds are killed every year by plastic rubbish that is in the ocean.

Who sleeps in a muddy bed?

Sea cucumbers do! These slug-like animals live in mud, eat mud and poo mud! Sea cucumbers are animals, not vegetables, but some people do like to eat them!

I'm a longnose sawshark. I hunt fish and crabs that are hiding in the mud. My nose is lined with sharp teeth!

The bottom of the sea is covered in mud and sand. It's called the seabed!

How do people explore under the sea?

People can't breathe in water, but we still find ways to explore the deep ocean. We can scuba dive, use submarines, or send robots with cameras.

I'm a glowing jellyfish called a mauve stinger.

Remotely operated underwater vehicles are one way for people to explore deep water from the safety of the surface

Who stands on three legs?

Tripod fish have three long, leg-like fins to stand on the seabed. Each fin-leg can be more than 50 centimetres long! Then they keep their mouths open and wait for food to swim right in.

Who lights up the deep, dark sea?

Sunlight can't reach the bottom of the deep sea. So some animals make their own light instead!

Viperfish like me use flashing lights to attract little animals to swim close. Then we swallow them up! My mouth is so big I can swallow animals bigger than me!

Puffin

Why does the sea go in and out?

Over the course of a day at the seaside you will see the sea moving in and out. This is called the tide, and it's caused by the Moon!

When the tide is in, the shore is covered with water. When the tide is out, there's still some water left in rock pools. How many animals can you see living here?

Why is there jelly in a rock pool?

Eel

Brittlestar

Goby

Hermit crab

I'm not jelly, I'm a beadlet anemone! When the tide is in, my tentacles wave in the water. When it goes out I fold my tentacles in so I look like a wobbly blob!

Who loves to surf?

Humans — but dolphins ride the waves too! Flat water turns to waves when wind blows over the top of it.

Which animals go to school?

We do! Young orcas like us have to learn to catch our lunch! Our mums take us to shallow water to show us how to hunt shoals of fish, seals and baby whales.

Lumpsucker

Who snacks at the shore?

Grey seals feed on all kinds of animals near the shore, from crabs to seabirds. They can also dive to depths of 70 metres when hunting.

Would you rather?

Which would you prefer — soaring with a **sea eagle** or surfing with a **penguin**?

I soar on 2-metre-wide wings, plucking sea snakes and turtles out of the water.

I use my wings like flippers to swim and leap through the waves.

My big mouth is full of eggs! After my mate lays them I keep them safe in my mouth until they hatch.

Would you rather be covered in spikes like a **pineapplefish** or have a huge mouth like a **jawfish**?

Would you rather be a **marine biologist** and study ocean animals, or a **marine geologist** and find out all about the mysterious seabed?

Would it be nicer to hold hands with a furry **sea otter**...

... or with a **blind hairy yeti crab**?

Is it better to have your feet nibbled by a **cleaner fish**, or tickled by a **feather duster worm**?

Would you rather have teeth as big as a **walrus's tusks**, or a long nose like a **sailfish**?

I'm the size of an elephant and consume 200 litres of milk a day!

...or as little as a **mother octopus**?

Would you like to eat as much as a **baby blue whale**...

I don't eat anything while I look after my eggs – and that can take eight months!

Who walks on water?

Polar bears do. They live in the Arctic Ocean. It's so cold there that the ocean freezes over.

Walruses and seals use their flippers to scoot over the Arctic ice before diving into the sea.

Why don't fish freeze?
Icefish have special blood that doesn't freeze – even if the water around them turns to ice!

Greenland sharks like me swim slowly to save energy in sub-zero temperatures.

Why do icebergs float?

Icebergs are made of frozen water. Ice is lighter than water, so it floats. Big sheets of ice float on the sea too. They are good places for penguins and seals to take a nap when they are tired of swimming, slipping and sliding!

Where did that seal go?

Under the ice – I'm brilliant at holding my breath! We Weddell seals only have to poke our heads up through holes in the ice once an hour to get air.

Who sings beautiful songs in the cold sea?

I do! I'm a white beluga whale and I sing so loudly that people in boats can hear my lovely songs.

Who packs a powerful punch?

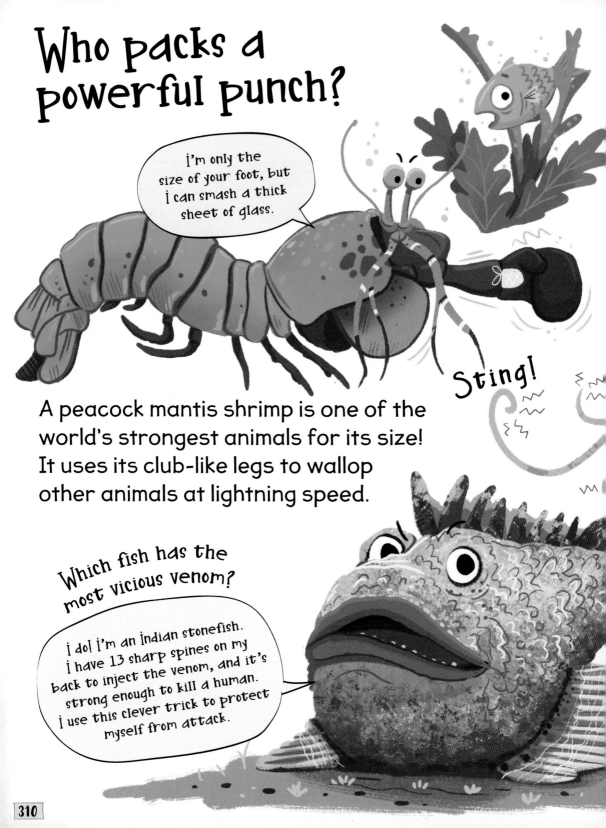

i'm only the size of your foot, but i can smash a thick sheet of glass.

Sting!

A peacock mantis shrimp is one of the world's strongest animals for its size! It uses its club-like legs to wallop other animals at lightning speed.

Which fish has the most vicious venom?

i do! i'm an indian stonefish. i have 13 sharp spines on my back to inject the venom, and it's strong enough to kill a human. i use this clever trick to protect myself from attack.

Why do jellyfish sting?

A jellyfish uses its long, stinging tentacles to get a meal. Each tentacle carries tiny, venomous darts that jab passing fish prey.

I'm a box jellyfish — the most dangerous jellyfish in the world. I have enough venom to kill 60 people!

Who can smell a drop of blood in the sea?

Sharks can! These incredible hunters have a super sense of smell that helps them find fish and other animals to eat.

Sniff!

Hammerhead sharks have strange heads. This odd shape helps us to see and smell animals, and to swim fast.

One tentacle can grow more than 20 metres long!

Are there monsters in the sea?

There are some very big animals in the sea... but no monsters. From huge rays and outsize crabs to the biggest animal on Earth — plenty of giants lurk in the deep.

Why do whales spout water?

That's how they breathe! Whales breathe air. They all have one or two blowholes, which are like nostrils. A spout from a whale is really just a big, warm, wet breath!

Which crab has the longest legs?

A Japanese spider crab has 10 legs, and each leg can be over 2 metres long! These mega crabs can reach 100 years old.

What's the biggest animal?

Me! I'm also the biggest animal to ever live! I can grow up 25 metres long and my tongue weighs the same as an elephant.

A compendium of questions

Can I drink seawater?

No – it can make you sick. Seawater is too salty, and often dirty too. The dirt is called pollution and it's bad for all living things.

Can I swim across an ocean?

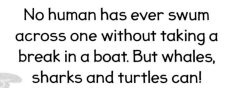

No human has ever swum across one without taking a break in a boat. But whales, sharks and turtles can!

Why do thresher sharks have such long tails?

They use the enormous upper lobes of their tail fins to wallop shoals of their fish prey.

Which fish ties itself in knots?

A hagfish! It's covered in slippery slime and ties itself in knots when it is feasting on dead animals at the bottom of the sea.

How smart is an octopus?

An octopus can work out how to open a jar to reach food inside! It uses its suckers to grip shellfish and rip them open.

Why is a blobfish so ugly?

I'm prettier underwater!

When a blobfish is brought to the surface of the sea its soft, spongy flesh goes floppy. When it is busy hunting in the deep sea it looks quite different.

Why does a firefly squid glow?

To hide, and to be seen! This squid can mimic the light above or below it if it wants to hide, and glow brightly when it wants to attract a mate.

Did that fish's eye just move?

Maybe! Baby flounders have an eye on each side of their head. As they grow, one eye moves to join the other — so the adult flounder can spend its days lying on the seafloor.

Which fish uses oars?

The fins of the strange, ribbon-like oarfish look a bit like oars. It's the longest bony fish — reaching up to 11 metres.

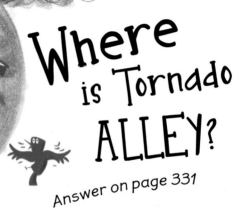

Where is Tornado ALLEY?

Answer on page 331

What makes water WONDERFUL?

Answer on page 320

Why DOES the wind blow?

Answer on page 326

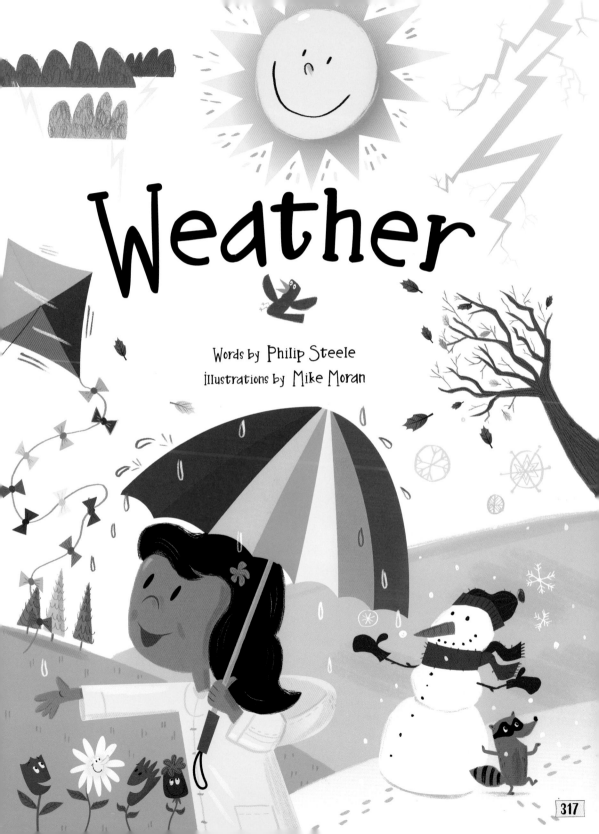

Weather

Words by Philip Steele

Illustrations by Mike Moran

What is weather?

Earth is surrounded by a layer of air called the atmosphere. The way the atmosphere behaves is always changing. It is these changes that give us the weather, which may be hot, cold, wet, windy or sunny.

Sun

Earth

Mind the wind doesn't blow your hat off!

The atmosphere is filled with moving air and clouds

South Pole

Why does weather happen?

The Sun is the nearest star to Earth. It is far, far away in space, but its incredible heat warms our planet. This warmth affects the way that air presses against Earth's surface. Differences between cold and warm places create strong winds, as well as currents in the oceans.

Why do seasons change?

As Earth travels around the Sun, it is tilted. This means that northern and southern parts lean towards the Sun at different times of the year. So when the north part is leaning towards the Sun it is summer there, and winter in the southern part.

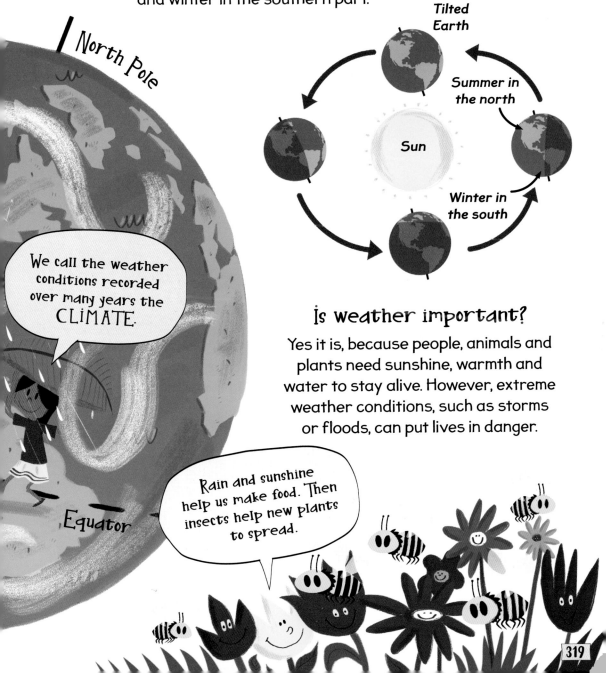

Tilted Earth

Summer in the north

Sun

Winter in the south

North Pole

We call the weather conditions recorded over many years the CLIMATE.

Equator

Is weather important?

Yes it is, because people, animals and plants need sunshine, warmth and water to stay alive. However, extreme weather conditions, such as storms or floods, can put lives in danger.

Rain and sunshine help us make food. Then insects help new plants to spread.

What makes water wonderful?

Water is a liquid. It can freeze to become solid ice. It can turn into a gas called water vapour. Water may change its form, but it lasts forever.

2 It gets gassy

Heat from the Sun turns water into a gas, called water vapour. This is **evaporation**.

1 There's lots of it!

Over **two thirds** of the Earth's surface is covered in water.

Water is precious

Fresh water keeps us **alive**. Water helps plants grow, too. We can wash in it, swim in it, sail on it, and play in it!

Whoosh!

Splash!

3 It rises and cools

As warm water vapour rises, it cools down. It **condenses**, turning back into liquid.

The higher you go, the colder it gets!

4 It makes clouds

Water droplets or solid ice crystals gather around specks of dust and form **clouds**.

5 It falls back down

Don't forget your umbrella!

Water droplets or ice crystals form **raindrops** or **snowflakes**, which fall back to Earth.

6 It goes on and on

Rain and melted snow fill rivers, lakes and oceans, then the whole **water cycle** starts all over again. It helps create our weather.

How hot does it get?

In California's Death Valley, the top temperature ever recorded was over 56°C. A weather satellite has recorded over 70°C in the Lut Desert in Iran.

We can measure temperature in degrees Celsius (°C). At the centre of the Sun it's about 15 million°C.

Where is the driest place on Earth?

The Atacama Desert in Chile. Once, no rain fell there for over 14 years. Long periods without rain are called droughts.

Atacama Desert

Why do lizards sunbathe?

Reptiles such as lizards are cold-blooded, which means that they can't make their own heat. They bask in the sunshine to warm themselves up.

Lizard

How can plants survive in a desert?

Some plants have their own water supply. Cacti store water in their thick, spiky stems. Baobab trees store water inside their big, fat trunks.

Cactus

Baobab tree

Why can the Sun be a danger?

The Sun can burn your skin and make you ill. On a sunny day, cover up your skin, wear a hat, slap on some sun cream and drink plenty of water.

Don't forget I need a drink too!

Where does the weather happen?

In the layer of the atmosphere that is closest to Earth's surface. The atmosphere surrounds our planet like a giant blanket, screening out some harmful rays that come from the Sun.

Atmosphere

Cumulonimbus

What is a weather system?

Huge masses of air that swirl over Earth's surface are called weather systems. High pressure systems press air down against the land. They bring drier, clearer weather. Low pressure systems bring mild or rainy weather. The border between two systems is called a front.

On TV, the weather is explained with maps and symbols.

Cirrus

Why do clouds have funny shapes?

Some clouds are white and puffy, some are thin and streaky. Some pile up like big dark towers, some form little blobs. Their shape depends on whether they are full of water droplets or ice crystals and how high up they are.

Some clouds look like dragons, castles or bears in the sky. What can you see up there?

Mackerel sky

Is there a pot of gold at the end of a rainbow?

Only in fairy tales! Rainbows are the most beautiful sights in the sky. Air has no colour, but when sunlight passes through rain or mist, the water droplets break up the light into an arc of shimmering colours.

Why does the wind blow?

Because as warm air rises, cold air whooshes in to take its place, and the wind blows! Some winds blow between land and sea. Some cross deserts and mountains. Others blow all the way around the planet.

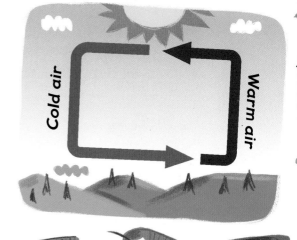

Cold air

Warm air

Sycamore seeds

How does the wind help plants?

Many trees and flowering plants have seeds that are scattered by the wind. Dandelion seeds are light and fluffy, and float a long way. Sycamore seeds are like helicopter blades, spinning around.

Dandelion seeds

What is the monsoon?

It is a wind that blows across India. The winter monsoon brings dry weather. In summer it picks up lots of water from the ocean and brings heavy rains to the dry land.

Summer monsoon can bring flooding.

Wandering albatross

Why do birds ride on the wind?

Condor

So we can fly long distances without too much flapping. Over the Southern Ocean, albatrosses like me glide on powerful winds. In South America, condors use currents of warm air to soar above mountains.

Pillar

How do winds shape rock?

Winds often carry dust, grit or sand. They blast rocks and cliffs, wearing them down into all sorts of shapes. Water, ice and heat also shape the surface of planet Earth.

Arch

Would you rather?

Go on holiday somewhere **cold** or somewhere **hot**?

Hear crashing **thunder** or see flashes of **lightning**?

BANG!

FLASH!

Play football in the **rain and mud** or during a **heatwave**?

Cruise by boat on a **calm day**...

...or sail on a **windy day**?

Fly **above** the clouds...

Sheep's wool contains lanolin, a grease that keeps out the rain.

Wear a **woolly coat** like a sheep, or a **green raincoat** like a tree frog?

I am covered in waterproof skin!

Ride on a **surfboard**...

...or a **snowboard**?

Work outside in a **big storm** at sea or inside designing a weather satellite for space?

...or drift **below** the clouds?

What is a hurricane?

It's a terrifying tropical storm, also called a typhoon or a cyclone. A great storm cloud spins around as it sweeps over the ocean. Hurricane-force winds can reach 180 kilometres an hour or even more.

The calm centre is called the 'eye' of the storm.

Is it deadly?

When a hurricane smashes into land it can be deadly. There are huge waves, heavy rain, floods and mudslides. Trees can be blown over, homes may be destroyed, and lives may be at risk.

Where is Tornado Alley?

This is an area in the United States that has some of the fiercest whirlwinds of all. They are called tornadoes or twisters. These dark funnels of dust can spin at up to 500 kilometres an hour. They can suck up a car or even a house.

WATCH OUT!

What is a waterspout?

A whirlwind that forms from warm, moist air over a sea or lake is called a waterspout. It is often joined to the bottom of a cloud.

Why are thunder clouds dark?

Thunder clouds are so full of water droplets that they look very dark. They tower up to 15 kilometres high.

How do clouds make lightning?

Water vapour rushes up into clouds from the warm ground. Once inside, the vapour cools and freezes, forming balls of ice called hailstones. Air currents ping these up and down inside the cloud, making an electric charge.

In a thunderstorm, stay away from water or metal fences.

BANG!

BOOM!

Thunderstorms can be dangerous.

Why does thunder go bang?

The heat of lightning is incredible, even hotter than the Sun. It makes the air expand so fast that it causes a shockwave. BANG!

Which comes first, thunder or lightning?

They happen at the same time, but we see the flash first because light travels through the air faster than sound.

How fast is lightning?

The electricity connects with the ground or with other clouds, forming a flash of lightning. This can travel 120,000 kilometres in a single second.

Go indoors if you can.

Do not stand under a tree.

Did you know?

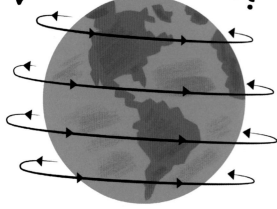

Super-powerful long-distance winds called **jet streams** rip along about 10 kilometres above the Earth's surface.

The Inuit people of the Arctic can build **igloos** — overnight shelters made from blocks of frozen snow. These are actually quite cosy!

It is said that no two **snowflakes** have exactly the same design!

Fog is just low-level cloud. The Grand Banks off Newfoundland, Canada, have about 206 foggy days each year.

As you are reading these words, there are about 2000 **thunderstorms** happening around the world.

The spinning of the Earth forces **winds** that blow from the Poles to the Equator to change direction.

COUGH!

When fumes from cars and factories react with sunlight, the air is filled with horrible, poisonous **smog**.

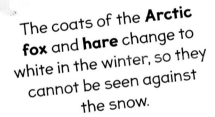

The coats of the **Arctic fox** and **hare** change to white in the winter, so they cannot be seen against the snow.

Fir trees have thin, tough leaves called **needles**, which stay on all winter. These help capture sunlight all year round. They can store water and survive harsh winter storms.

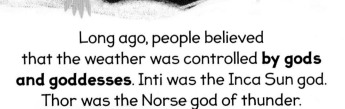

Long ago, people believed that the weather was controlled **by gods and goddesses**. Inti was the Inca Sun god. Thor was the Norse god of thunder.

How are snowflakes formed?

When water droplets freeze around specks of dust in a cloud, snowflakes form. These ice crystals freeze more droplets, building up amazing starry shapes and patterns. They stick together to make bigger flakes.

Snowflakes have SIX sides, or points.

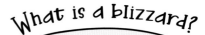
What is a blizzard?

A blizzard is a heavy snow storm driven by high winds. Snow piles up in deep drifts. It's hard to see where you are going as everything looks white!

Why are mountaintops snowy?

Mountaintops are often covered in snow, even in hot countries. The higher you climb, the more the air expands and cools. This leads to more moisture — and snowy mountain conditions.

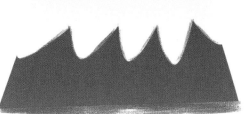

Where does frost make flowers?

On cold surfaces such as windows, ice or rock. Ice crystals spread into beautiful patterns, which look like ferns or flowers.

DANGER THIN ICE!

Does the sea ever freeze?

Yes it does, but because the sea contains salt, it has a lower freezing point. It turns to ice below -2° Celsius. Freshwater rivers and lakes freeze at 0° Celsius.

How many?

The number of days it once rained non-stop on the Hawaiian Island of Oahu!

332

4000
The number of hours of sunshine that Yuma, Arizona, USA receives in a year. It may be the sunniest place on Earth!

The biggest tropical storm ever recorded was a typhoon named Tip, in 1979. It measured **2220** kilometres across.

5 years!

That's how long a water-holding frog can go without water during a drought!

11.5 metres: The amount of snow that fell at Tamarack in California, USA, during just one day in 1911.

321
The number of kilometres a single lightning streak ran across the sky above Oklahoma, USA in 2007.

207
The number of tornadoes that happened in a single day in the USA in 2011.

8 hours **58** minutes:
The longest-lasting rainbow in Taiwan, in 2017.

1
The weight in kilograms of giant hailstones that fell in Bangladesh in 1986.

−89.2° Celsius.
The lowest temperature ever recorded was at the Vostok scientific base in Antarctica, in July 1983.

BRRRR!

How do we measure the weather?

All sorts of clever gadgets have been invented over the years to measure how the weather behaves. Today, the numbers are often recorded and displayed digitally.

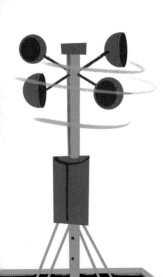

Anemometers measure wind speed. They are often fixed to tall buildings, bridges and ships.

Rain gauges collect and measure the amount of rain that falls into a jar.

Thermometers measure how hot or cold it gets. The best known thermometers show how a liquid metal called mercury goes up or down inside a glass tube. Most weather scientists today use electrical resistance thermometers.

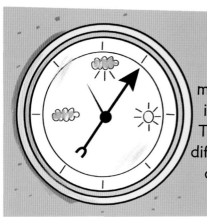

Barometers measure changes in air pressure. There are many different designs and displays.

Satellites

Satellites in space help us collect information about the climate. Buoys and ships at sea also record weather data, and so do aircraft.

Weather balloons carry instruments high above Earth to study the atmosphere.

Buoy

Weather science is called meteorology.

A compendium of questions

Why is rain sometimes red?

If rain gets mixed with sand picked up by desert winds, it can be red or orange.

Hi, I'm Katrina!

Hi, I'm Mitch!

Why are hurricanes given names?

It's an easy way of remembering which was which. Famous tropical storms have been called Katrina, Maria, Mitch and David.

Why do crocodiles like tropical storms?

If it floods, crocodiles can go hunting in the high street. You'd better watch out!

Where is there a special snow festival?

It is held each year in Sapporo, Japan. People make amazing statues and sculptures from ice and snow.

Why do people build houses on stilts?

When it floods in the rainy season in Assam, India, the houses stay high and dry.

Which countries have the worst floods?

India, Bangladesh and China have had some of the worst floods. This is due to heavy rains, melting snow from high mountains, big rivers and tropical storms.

Can it really rain frogs or fishes?

Yes! Tiny fish and frogs are sometimes sucked out of ponds and puddles, then fall back to land when it rains.

How do desert animals stay cool?

Many animals burrow underground and only come out at night, when it's cooler. The big ears of the fennec fox help its body to lose heat.

Where are rivers used as roads?

Winters are so cold in Siberia, Russia, that heavy trucks can drive along frozen rivers instead of roads. Milk is sold in solid slabs.

WHAT is a CARBON FOOTPRINT?

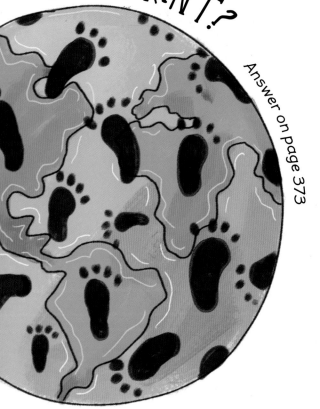

Answer on page 373

Where does WEE go?

Answer on page 358

How can we create less RUBBISH?

Answer on page 369

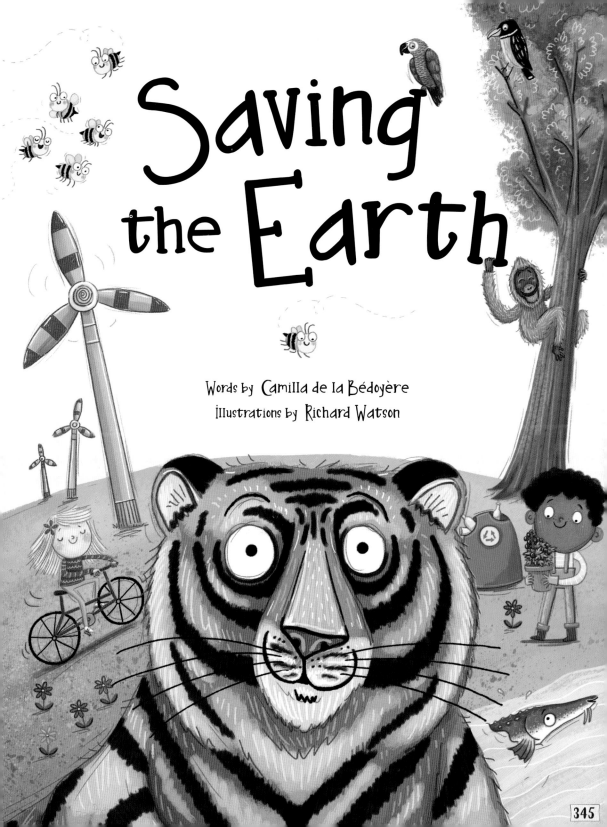

Saving the Earth

Words by Camilla de la Bédoyère

Illustrations by Richard Watson

Why is our planet in peril?

Our beautiful planet is in peril because we haven't been taking good care of it. Earth is a precious home for all of us, and the plants and animals that live here too.

How many people are on the planet?

There are more than 7.7 billion people. That's 7,700,000,000 humans! Every one of us has an important job to do. Let's work together to save the Earth!

What is air?

The air is made up of gases and it's wrapped around Earth like a snug blanket. It's called the atmosphere.

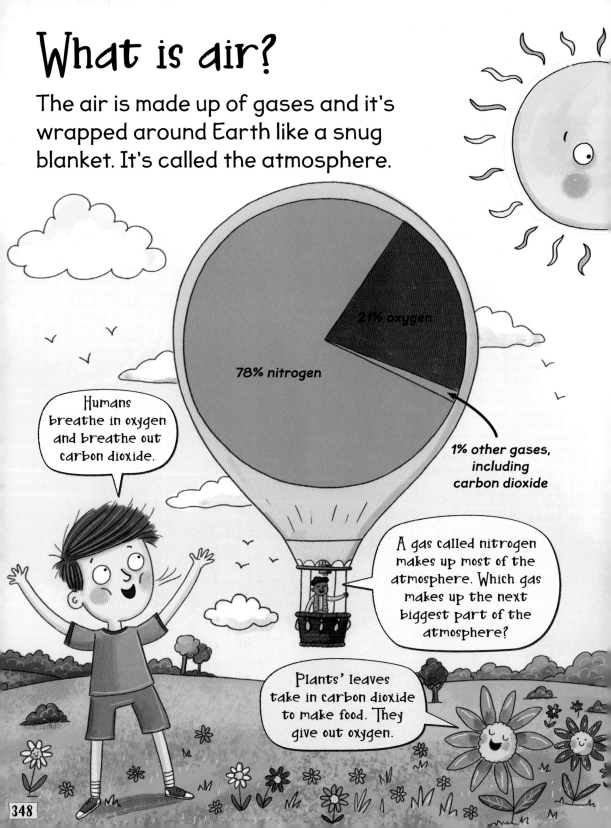

21% oxygen

78% nitrogen

1% other gases, including carbon dioxide

Humans breathe in oxygen and breathe out carbon dioxide.

A gas called nitrogen makes up most of the atmosphere. Which gas makes up the next biggest part of the atmosphere?

Plants' leaves take in carbon dioxide to make food. They give out oxygen.

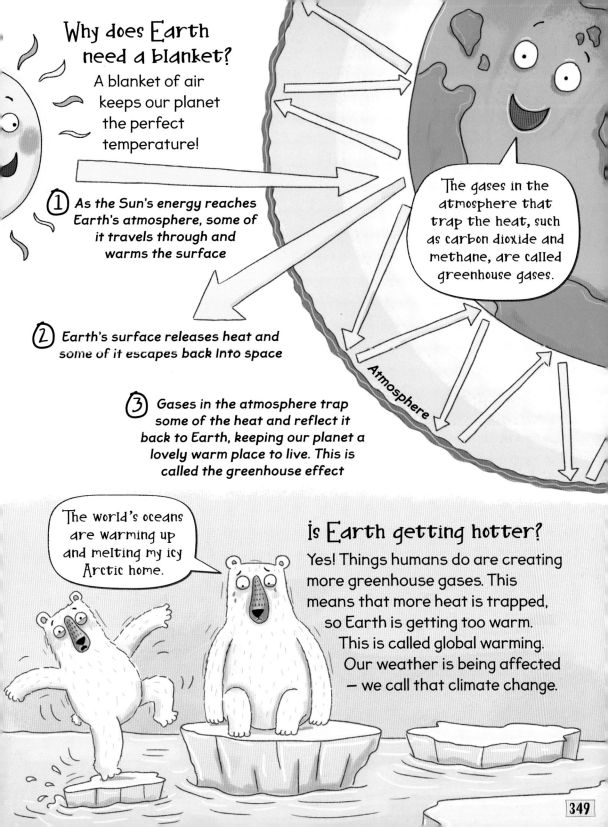

Why does Earth need a blanket?

A blanket of air keeps our planet the perfect temperature!

① As the Sun's energy reaches Earth's atmosphere, some of it travels through and warms the surface

② Earth's surface releases heat and some of it escapes back into space

③ Gases in the atmosphere trap some of the heat and reflect it back to Earth, keeping our planet a lovely warm place to live. This is called the greenhouse effect

The gases in the atmosphere that trap the heat, such as carbon dioxide and methane, are called greenhouse gases.

Atmosphere

The world's oceans are warming up and melting my icy Arctic home.

Is Earth getting hotter?

Yes! Things humans do are creating more greenhouse gases. This means that more heat is trapped, so Earth is getting too warm. This is called global warming. Our weather is being affected — we call that climate change.

Did you know?

Carbon dioxide

Plants are great at mopping up extra carbon dioxide and pumping lots of oxygen into the air! That's why we need forests, fields and parks.

Oxygen

If we didn't have an atmosphere there would be no air to breathe, and Earth's average temperature would be a very chilly -6°C!

There are more than one billion cows in the world, and almost all of them are kept on farms. They all make greenhouse gases when they fart and burp.

Sometimes Earth is called the Goldilocks planet because its distance from the Sun means it's just the right temperature for us.

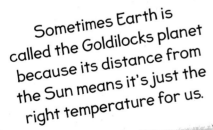

Too hot!

Just right!

Too cold!

5000 TODAY!

You can plant a tree to help keep Earth's atmosphere healthy. Some trees are more than 5000 years old.

Scientists looked at how hot the Earth was in the last 100 years and found the five hottest years have been since 2010.

Trees can be used to make all of these things: soap, shampoo, rubber gloves, chocolate, paper, clothes and medicines. When trees are cut down, it's important that new ones are planted.

Plants make perfect presents for people who care about the planet!

If you lined up all the cars in the world they could stretch round it 40 times! Think of all the dirty gases they are putting in the air, and leave your car at home whenever you can!

Trains are a greener way to travel than planes because they make up to six times less dirty gas.

We are taking too many fish from the sea. Some fishing nets are more than 60 metres wide and can trap tens of thousands of fish at a time.

What is dirty energy?

Burning oil, gas, wood and coal gives us energy to power our homes and vehicles. This puts more greenhouse gases in the air, and causes pollution.

Pollution is something in the environment that is harmful or poisonous.

Oil, gas and coal are called fossil fuels because they formed inside Earth long ago, from dead animals and plants!

Smoke containing harmful gases

This power station is burning coal. Most air pollution comes from burning fossil fuels

How can bikes help us save the planet?

Cycling, skate-boarding and walking are clean, green ways to get around. You can travel one kilometre by bike in about three minutes, by skateboard in about six minutes, or on foot in about 10 minutes.

This cycle lane is made up of solar panels. They use the Sun's energy to make electricity for lots of people.

Solar panels

What is clean energy?

Not all power comes from dirty fossil fuels. The great news is that there are loads of ways of making clean, green energy!

Wind turbines can turn wind energy into electricity, or other types of power

Wind power

The energy of flowing water can be used to make hydroelectric power

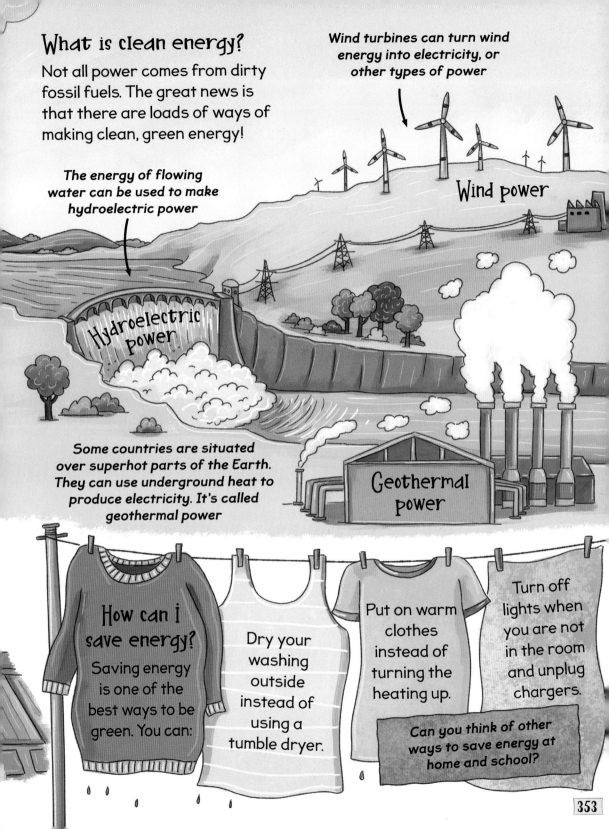

Hydroelectric power

Some countries are situated over superhot parts of the Earth. They can use underground heat to produce electricity. It's called geothermal power

Geothermal power

How can I save energy?

Saving energy is one of the best ways to be green. You can:

Dry your washing outside instead of using a tumble dryer.

Put on warm clothes instead of turning the heating up.

Turn off lights when you are not in the room and unplug chargers.

Can you think of other ways to save energy at home and school?

Why are jellyfish blooming?

Jellyfish love warm water, and as the world's oceans get warmer, the number of jellyfish is rising. Large numbers can even form massive groups, or blooms. The fish aren't so happy, as jellyfish eat them!

Seals that normally eat the fish now have less food. The damage we do to our planet affects all living things.

Why did my colourful home turn white?

Coral reefs need clean, warm water to survive. When the water gets too hot, or dirty, the coral animals die, and the reef turns white.

Why are the oceans dirty?

Our oceans are dirtier than ever because lots of plastic waste has been dumped in the water. Plastic in the ocean gets broken down into tiny pieces, and animals eat them.

Join a seaside clean-up to help keep beaches clean.

Always take your rubbish home and recycle as much of it as you can.

Ask for paper straws instead of plastic ones, which often end up in the sea.

How can I help turtles?

Some turtles try to eat plastic bags floating in the sea. They think the bags are their favourite food — jellyfish — and the plastic kills them.

You can help us turtles and other sea creatures by using canvas or long-life shopping bags instead of plastic ones.

When you go on holiday, don't buy souvenirs that are made from animals or their homes.

How many?

More than **80** countries already use wind power to produce electricity.

In Japan, people use wooden chopsticks to eat. Every year, they get through **90,000** tonnes of them! Can you think of some fun ways to reuse chopsticks?

1

The number of drinks cans you need to recycle to save energy for **4** hours of TV.

There is so much heat deep inside Earth that it could provide us with enough power for **1,000,000** years!

Make sure all your light bulbs are the new energy-saving ones. They last up to **15** times longer and can be recycled!

640

The number of litres of water a garden sprinkler uses in an hour. Use a watering can instead!

85% of the world's energy still comes from fossil fuels, although many people are working hard to reduce this. Are you?

100
The number of trees you could save from being cut down if your whole class recycle paper for a year.

It takes **50** times as much energy to make a battery as there is stored in the battery! Use rechargeable batteries whenever you can.

The Great Pacific Garbage Patch, a mass of litter floating in the North Pacific Ocean, covers around **1.6 million** square kilometres.

Pacific Ocean

10

The number of litres of clean water in a toilet flush.

Only **3%** of the water on Earth is fresh (not salty), and most of that is frozen. This is why we need to save water where we can.

Where does wee go?

All of the waste water from our homes gets carried away in underground pipes. They're called sewers.

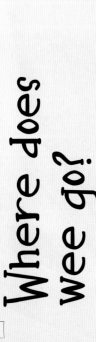

Why are showers best?

A bath uses about 80 litres of water, but a shower uses about 40 litres instead.

Cleaning water uses lots of energy. Turn off the tap while you are brushing your teeth. Can you think of other ways to save water?

That stinks!

Sewers carry the waste water to a place where it is cleaned so it can be used again

Some sewers also collect rainwater. If the sewer overflows, it empties into rivers or the ocean!

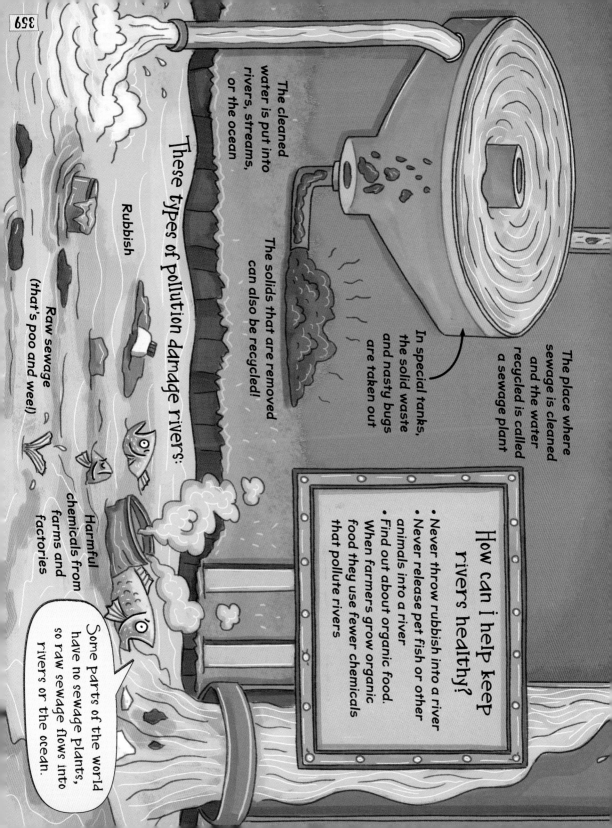

The place where
sewage is cleaned
and the water
recycled is called
a sewage plant

The cleaned
water is put into
rivers, streams,
or the ocean

In special tanks,
the solid waste
and nasty bugs
are taken out

The solids that are removed
can also be recycled!

These types of pollution damage rivers:

Rubbish

Raw sewage
(that's poo and wee!)

Harmful
chemicals from
farms and
factories

How can I help keep
rivers healthy?

• Never throw rubbish into a river
• Never release pet fish or other
  animals into a river
• Find out about organic food.
  When farmers grow organic
  food they use fewer chemicals
  that pollute rivers

Some parts of the world
have no sewage plants,
so raw sewage flows into
rivers or the ocean.

How far did my banana travel?

The distance food travels from where it was grown, to where it will be eaten, is measured in food miles.

2 Then it crossed an ocean

5000 miles

4 We bought it and it travelled in our car to get to our home

5 miles

1 This banana travelled by truck to get to a boat

50 miles

3 Then it was put on a lorry and taken to a supermarket

70 miles

5 It came with me on my bike to school

2 miles

How many food miles does this banana have? Which part of its journey used the least energy?

Why are worms really useful?

We munch up leftover food, peelings, eggshells and garden waste. We turn it into compost.

I put the compost on my garden to help new plants grow. Thanks worms!

Who has green fingers?

I do! I grow fruit and veg in my garden so these foods have no food miles!

How can food waste be turned into energy?

When food rots it gives off methane. This can be collected and used for cooking, or heating homes. Plant waste can also be used to make fuel for cars.

1 Food waste is collected from homes, supermarkets and restaurants.

2 All the waste goes in a special sealed tank, where no oxygen can reach it

3 Bacteria in the tank eat the waste, which gives off methane as it breaks down

Methane can also be collected from my poo!

4 The methane is used to power electricity generators

5 Electricity is supplied to homes

Would you rather?

Would you rather save water by sharing a **bath** with your dog, or by giving yourself a time limit on your **showers**?

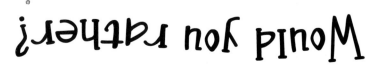

If you get cold, would you rather warm up by **running** on the spot or by wearing a big **jumper**?

You want to recycle your old toys. Would you rather take them to a **charity shop**, or **swap** them with a friend?

Would you rather be a wriggly worm eating **rotten food** in a compost heap, or a dung beetle munching on **elephant poo**?

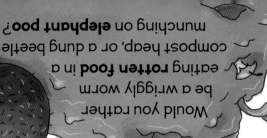

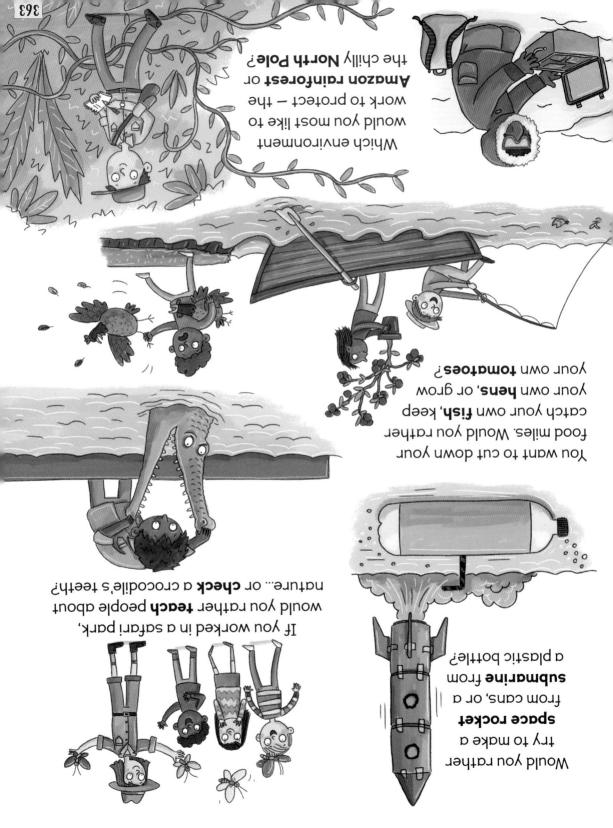

Which environment would you most like to work to protect — the **Amazon rainforest** or the chilly **North Pole**?

You want to cut down your food miles. Would you rather catch your own **fish**, keep your own **hens**, or grow your own **tomatoes**?

If you worked in a safari park, would you rather **teach** people about nature... or **check** a crocodile's teeth?

Would you rather try to make a **space rocket** from cans, or a **submarine** from a plastic bottle?

What is an animal's home called?

The place where an animal lives is called a habitat. Forests, grasslands, rivers and deserts are types of habitat. When habitats are destroyed, some animals lose their homes, and might go extinct.

Bengal tiger

How can you help to save animal habitats?

Wildlife charities work to save habitats, and raising money for them is a good way to help. It's also a good idea to only buy food and products that have been made without harming wild habitats.

I'm doing a sponsored silence to raise money to protect wild habitats.

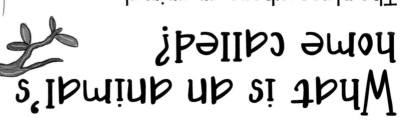

Bornean orangutan

Where did your home go?

In Borneo, diverse forests the size of 180 football pitches are cut down every hour so palm trees can be grown. Avoid buying foods made with palm oil and you can help us keep our homes.

What causes extinction?

Extinction is when a type of animal or plant dies out so there are none left on Earth. There are lots of reasons for extinction, but today humans are doing so much damage to the world that we are putting many animals at risk.

Going...
Beluga sturgeons are under threat because they are fished for their valuable eggs

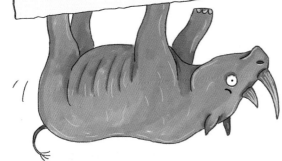

Going...
Rhinos are hunted and killed because some people want their horns

Gone
Golden toads probably went extinct because of global warming

Why are rainforests important?

Rainforests are home to billions of animals and plants. When rainforest trees are burned to clear the land for farming, they release carbon dioxide. That makes climate change worse.

Sun bear

Where does all the rubbish go?

When we throw rubbish away we sort it into different bins. Some of it will end up in landfill or being burned, which is very bad for the environment. It's better to go zero! That means trying to create no rubbish at all.

Some of this rubbish will never rot. It will stay in the ground for hundreds, or even thousands of years.

What's that stink?

A landfill is a huge hole in the ground where rubbish is put. As the rubbish rots, it gives off methane. It's a more harmful greenhouse gas than carbon dioxide.

Painted turtles

Grasshopper sparrow

Osprey

How can rubbish turn green?

Freshkills, in the USA, was once the world's biggest landfill. Now it's being turned into a park and more than 200 types of animal live there.

Why is rubbish a hot topic?

This rubbish is hot — burning hot! It's being burned in a big oven, called an incinerator. The rubbish is burned instead of being put into landfill. As it burns, it releases lots of pollution.

Five hundred steel cans can be recycled to build a bike!

How can I go zero?

If you recycle, or reuse, all your rubbish you have gone zero! Turn the page to discover how recycling and reusing helps to reduce the amount of rubbish that goes to landfill, or is burned.

What are the three Rs?

Reduce, Reuse and Recycle! By cutting down the amount of energy we use and waste we create, we can help to make Earth a better place.

REDUCE
Cutting down the amount of meat you eat can cut greenhouse gases.

REUSE
Using paper more than once means fewer trees will be cut down – and save a forest.

RECYCLE
You can save energy by recycling. That helps protect Earth's atmosphere from damage.

Use a toothbrush made from bamboo, not plastic.

Carry your lunch in reusable tubs or beeswax wrappers instead of plastic wrap.

Plastic can be difficult to recycle, so try not to buy things that come in lots of plastic packaging.

Use a reusable water bottle and fill it with tap water.

How can we create less rubbish?

The solid sludge that is collected at sewage farms can be turned into fertiliser. Farmers put it on their fields to help plants grow.

Elephant, rhino and kangaroo poo can be used to make paper.

Llama poo can be burned on fires to keep people warm, or cook their food

Can poo be recycled?

Yes it can!

What are we doing to save the planet?

All over the world, people are working hard to save the planet for your future — at home, on farms and in the workplace. Saving the planet is a job for everyone.

What is conservation?
Conservation is the work people do to protect wild and special places.

We collect wood to burn at home, for cooking and heating, but we are planting new trees to replace the wood we use.

My job is to look after the Great Barrier Reef and teach people about the animals that live here.

I live in the Amazon rainforest. I take care of this precious habitat so it will still be here for my children and grandchildren.

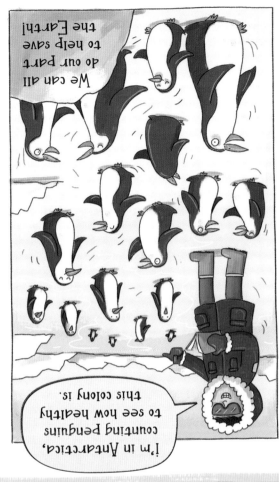

We can all do our part to help save the Earth!

I'm in Antarctica, counting penguins to see how healthy this colony is.

What's a solar farm?

A solar farm is a place with lots of solar panels. The panels collect sunlight and turn it into electricity.

The largest solar farms are in hot countries. They have more than 2 million solar panels.

I'm a solar-powered cleaning machine! At this solar farm in India, we keep the panels clear of sand so they can keep soaking up the sunlight.

A compendium of questions

How can I feed wild birds?
You can grow flowers that will make seeds for the birds to eat in winter. You can also buy bird food and hang it from trees in bird feeders.

How can I use less plastic?
Think about whether you need to buy a product in plastic. Liquid soap, for example, comes in plastic bottles, but a bar of soap is wrapped in paper.

It's a good idea to fill up a bird bath, or leave a bowl of water out so birds can drink and wash – far from any place where cats can hide!

What can I do for nature on a day out?
Enjoy looking at plants and animals, but avoid picking flowers or disturbing animal homes. Always take your rubbish home.

What should I do with old clothes?
Clothes can be recycled, they can be cut up and used as rags for cleaning, or if they are in good condition you can sell or swap them, or take them to charity shops.

What's a swap-shop?

Instead of throwing things out, you can swap them! Set up a swap-shop where people can bring toys or books they have finished using, and trade them for something someone else has donated.

How can I make an animal habitat?

Make a pile of logs, sticks and leaves in a shady place outside. Bugs and small animals will be happy to make their home there.

Can I make gifts instead of buying them?

Making gifts is a great way to reuse and recycle. You could turn old greetings cards into bookmarks and gift tags.

What type of gift keeps on giving?

A plant! You can grow a tomato or bean plant from seed and give it to someone else.

What is a carbon footprint?

It is a measure of how much carbon dioxide is released into the atmosphere because of how you live your life. Cutting our carbon footprint will help in the battle against climate change.

index